THE LOGIC OF
CONCEPT EXPANSION

MEIR BUZAGLO

CAMBRIDGE
UNIVERSITY PRESS

PUBLISHED BY THE PRESS SYNDICATE OF THE UNIVERSITY OF CAMBRIDGE
The Pitt Building, Trumpington Street, Cambridge, United Kingdom

CAMBRIDGE UNIVERSITY PRESS
The Edinburgh Building, Cambridge CB2 2RU, UK
40 West 20th Street, New York, NY 10011-4211, USA
477 Williamstown Road, Port Melbourne, VIC 3207, Australia
Ruiz de Alarcón 13, 28014 Madrid, Spain
Dock House, The Waterfront, Cape Town 8001, South Africa

http://www.cambridge.org

First published 2002

Printed in the United Kingdom at the University Press, Cambridge

Typeface Baskerville Monotype 11/12.5 pt.   *System* LATEX 2$_\varepsilon$ [TB]

A catalogue record for this book is available from the British Library

Library of Congress Cataloguing in Publication data
Buzaglo, Meir, 1959–
The Logic of Concept Expansion / by Meir Buzaglo.
p.   cm.
Includes bibliographical references and index.
ISBN 0 521 80762 X
1. Logic.   2. Concepts.   I. Title.
BC199.C55 B89   2001
160 – dc21   2001037558

ISBN 0 521 80762 x hardback

THE LOGIC OF CONCEPT EXPANSION

Scientists and mathematicians frequently describe the development of their field as a process that includes the expansion of concepts. Logicians traditionally deny the possibility of conceptual expansion and the coherence of this description. Meir Buzaglo's innovative study proposes a way of expanding logic to include the stretching of concepts, while modifying the principles which apparently block this possibility. He offers stimulating discussions of the idea of conceptual expansion as a normative process, and of the relation of conceptual expansion to truth, meaning, reference, ontology and paradox. He analyzes the views of Kant, Wittgenstein, Gödel, and others, paying especially close attention to Frege. His book will be of interest to a wide range of readers, from philosophers (of logic, mathematics, language, and science) to logicians, mathematicians, linguists, and cognitive scientists.

MEIR BUZAGLO is Lecturer at the Department of Philosophy in the Hebrew University of Jerusalem. He is the author of *Solomon Maimon's Metaphysics: A Reconstruction* (Pittsburgh University Press, forthcoming).

To the memory
of my brother Raphael

Contents

Preface

Two issues have interested me for a long time. One is Kant's perception of metaphysics as an illusion-prone area, while the other involves the intriguing way mathematicians expand their concepts. Although mathematicians may talk about the sine of a complex number, they do not try to define the sine function to apply to the moon. The connection between the two areas becomes clearer when one recalls that Kant has argued that the antinomies of reason derive from illegitimate expansions of concepts beyond their range of application (e.g., applying the categories of causality to the whole world of phenomena). It is important to note that this connection has reappeared and even intensified in contemporary thought. One cannot imagine modern mathematics and physics without the procedure of expansions of concepts, and the analyses of Russell's paradoxes by Russell, Gödel, and others are echoes of Kant's view that one cannot view certain totalities as genuine objects. A parallel approach, with certain changes, may even be attributed to Wittgenstein, whose aim in philosophy was to "bring words back home," as well as Brouwer's diagnosis that classical logic was derived from a careless expansion of logical laws that are valid for finite collections to unbounded ranges.

These developments raise an interesting question about Kant's analysis of the source of illusions, as they make it clear that modern scientists and mathematicians do not respect the boundaries within which the concepts they use were originally defined. It even seems as if they take the opposite tack, expanding whenever possible. To put it differently, while philosophical disillusionment with metaphysics seemed to demand restraint, scientists kept pushing at the borders of meaning, trying to go beyond the accepted sense of terms.

All this implies that the fact that philosophers projected their words beyond their original use does not suffice to render their efforts as mere illusion. We should therefore either improve the Kantian picture on antinomies or reject it. For example, it is clear that the expansion of causality on the world as a whole is of a different kind than expanding the sine function to the moon; expansions in philosophy seem more natural. Could we therefore view them as expansions in science? Having formulated this question, I had to face another difficulty, for I did not have a frame of reference that would allow me to connect a phenomenon from the sciences to pure metaphysics. By this I do not mean that I could not generalize this process and suggest a logic wherein one could analyze and classify expansions, but what I lacked was a philosophical standpoint that would help me to judge matters better.

At this point I discovered Frege's opposition to the whole idea of expanding concepts. Frege's rejection was grounded in the main principles of his system. These principles served as a middle term and have allowed me to connect a phenomenon from mathematics to general questions on meaning and reference, and to start a new train of thought. Thus, in contrast to Frege's position, I am convinced that the phenomenon of expansions is essential to concepts, and in the concluding chapters I show that the notion of a dichotomy between meaningful and meaningless sentences is inconclusive (although this is not directly connected with the issue of vagueness). This allows me to return to my original question on the way natural non-arbitrary expansions lead us to antinomies, and, what is even more important, to uncover a prevalent logical form that may be applicable to other areas which I delineate in the introduction to this book.

Having finished the book I realize that there are many issues I have left open. What I would most like to do is to analyze Putnam's position on conceptual change, which is a major axis of his thought, as well as the role of expansions in Quine's views, and it would be interesting to read some of Wittgenstein's writings in light of my present suggestions. The reason I do not go into these issues here is that I prefer to develop the instrument proposed here as far as possible before confronting it with more mature philosophies. From this standpoint, the present book is a preparation for a richer dialogue, as well as an introduction to a better understanding of the above-mentioned philosophers.

Acknowledgments

I would like to thank a number of teachers and friends. For my interest in Frege I am indebted to my teacher and mentor Gilead Bar-Elli. Without Frege I would not have had a worthy opponent against whom to construct my present view, and without Gilead I would not have been intrigued by Frege. (This does not mean, of course, that Gilead accepts my criticism of Frege.)

Saharon Shelah helped me prove two theorems about the logic of expansions that are presented here. Even though it was not very difficult for him (I can attest that it took him no more than five minutes), it saved me a great deal of hard work.

I began the work leading to this book at Harvard, in the company of Hilary Putnam, and I am very lucky to have benefited from his encouragement and guidance. At the Hebrew University I was fortunate in being able to study in two of its excellent departments. In the Department of Mathematics I studied logic, and I began my investigations of the logic of changes in extension under the guidance of Menachem Magidor. In the Department of Philosophy I also received much advice and encouragement. Mark Steiner encouraged me to work on the present book. Carl Posy helped me with his generous attentiveness, and thanks to him I was able to improve the presentation of my research. Yemima Ben-Menachem read drafts of my work and made helpful comments. The students in my seminars at the Hebrew University also helped me a great deal, most especially Hilly Razinsky and Gall Elster. This research was supported by the Israel Science Foundation, founded by the Israel Academy of Sciences and Humanities.

I would like to thank Dr. Naomi Goldblum not only for translating this book from Hebrew but also for helping me with useful suggestions. If the text is clear, it is due to her efforts.

Finally, my very special thanks go to my wife, Dina, whose support gave me the courage to work on this book.

Introduction

The concept of square root was expanded to include the negative numbers; the concept of power, originally defined only for the natural numbers, was expanded to include zero, fractions, and real and complex numbers; the logarithm function, which was originally defined only for positive numbers, was expanded to the negative numbers; in general, nearly every mathematical function has been expanded in a non-arbitrary way. But this is not only true of mathematics; in physics as well there are expansions of concepts that were originally defined only for a restricted range. The expansion of the concept of temperature to black holes, the notion of instantaneous velocity, the idea of imaginary time, and perhaps even the idea of determining the age of the universe are a few examples of this process. Metaphors and analogies can also be considered expansions of concepts beyond the sphere in which they were first used. Moreover, philosophy has always been suspected of expanding concepts beyond their legitimate range of applicability. It seems that every area that contains concepts also contains expansions of concepts.

Various incidental remarks about expansions of concepts that have taken place throughout the development of modern mathematics were made by Leibniz, Pascal, Bernoulli, and Gauss. The first attempts to deal with this phenomenon systematically, however, were George Peacock's (1791–1858) "principle of permanence of equivalent forms" and Peano's requirement that logical notation must leave room for functions to develop. With Frege a crucial turn took place. Frege took the phenomenon of expansions more seriously than any other logician, but his conclusion was unfavorable:

It is all the more necessary to emphasize that logic cannot recognize as concepts quasi-conceptual constructions that are still fluid and have not yet been given definitive and sharp boundaries (Frege 1977a, vol. II, sec. 58).

Frege's opposition to the idea of expansions stemmed from his broad view of logic, based on the major principles that apply to linguistic expressions pertaining to science rather than fiction. And yet, in spite of Frege's objections, there is still a great deal of interest in the idea of expansions among logicians (e.g., Gödel, Hilbert, Robinson), model theorists, philosophers of mathematics (e.g., Lakatos), and general philosophers, most prominently Wittgenstein. Nevertheless, within the realm of logic, as far as it can be seen as an investigation of general rational principles and a discipline involving truth and language, one can say that Frege's view is still predominant. This book is an attempt to provide a systematic analysis of one type of non-arbitrary expansion of concepts, while taking Frege's objections into account.

Let us consider the expansion of the power function to include zero. This function was originally defined on the natural numbers as an abbreviation for the process of multiplying a number by itself n times, so how can we even consider what 2 to the "zeroth" power might be? The question is clearly odd, since it violates the very definition of the power function as an abbreviation of multiplication, and yet we have succeeded in giving the expression "2^0" a meaning. In order to do this, we have considered the laws that apply to the power function and expanded them to the present case. Thus we define $2^0 = 1$ because this is the only way to preserve these laws.

Another example is the expansion of the concept of number to infinite sets. This expansion, like the previous one, does not involve adding elements to the universe, as does the case of expanding the set of numbers to include the negative or the complex numbers.[1] In the present case it is the function "the number of elements in a set" that is expanded to include sets that are already known to exist on the basis of our axioms. The result of this expansion is the arithmetic of infinite numbers, which is a *sine qua non* for modern mathematics.

Now it may be possible to place metaphors, analogies, and vague concepts outside the realm of logic, as Frege does, but it is definitely undesirable to present a theory of logic in which this is the fate of the expansion of concepts of the sort illustrated here, since it is impossible to imagine modern mathematics and physics without such expansions. Here is the general structure of the argument I present in this book. While Frege claims that the idea of expansions detracts from the principles

---

[1] The reader might object at this point by claiming that the expansion of the notion of cardinal number is not of the same kind as the expansion of the power function. I discuss this issue in chapter 3.

of reference and sense, and that therefore there cannot be a logic that includes this process, I claim that there can be a logic that includes non-arbitrary expansions, and that there are convincing reasons to believe that a certain type of expansion expresses human rationality. Therefore, instead of allowing some principles to place this phenomenon outside logic, the principles must be changed so as to include this process. These changes will eventuate in a different conception of logic that is not confined to a general study of the space of reference and truth *after* they have already been consolidated, but also includes an analysis of how this space is established.

The first chapter of the present book describes some important milestones in the discussion of non-arbitrary expansions of concepts that preceded Frege's view. Expansions, as noted by Felix Klein (1939), have forced themselves on mathematicians since the sixteenth century, compelling them to give up the rigid standards they had inherited from the Greek mathematicians. Philosophers such as Leibniz used terms like "fiction" to describe what was happening, but this was insufficient. During the nineteenth century, when rigor gradually resumed a place of importance in mathematics, there was a systematic attempt to conceptualize the idea of expansions, as presented in Peacock's "principle of permanence of equivalent forms." This attempt transferred the issue from the products of the expansion to the *process* of expansion itself. Peacock claimed that the symbolic algebra obtained from the expansion of arithmetic is logically independent of arithmetic, yet suggested by it. How an expansion of a realm can be "suggested" by the existing realm has not, however, been analyzed properly. Apparently this lack is due to the fact that discussions in logic are generally centered on deduction, which involves closed realms, thus marginalizing the issue of the expansion of concepts. But the most cursory survey shows that there is an abundance of logical, mathematical, and philosophical material that is continually raising the idea of expansions as a logical and philosophical issue which naturally invites a more comprehensive discussion.

Frege was aware of these attempts to conceptualize the process of expansions through the work of Hankel and Peano, but he nevertheless rejected the entire notion of forced expansions. Chapter 2 discusses Frege's objections, extracting three arguments from his criticism of the legitimacy of the expansion of concepts. The first argument is based on Frege's mathematical realism, the second on his principle that concepts must be defined everywhere, and the third on his extensionalism. The third argument claims that if sentences are to be analyzed into components that refer to things in such a way that the truth-value of any sentence is a function of what its components denote, then the idea of the development of concepts must be rejected. This last argument is the most important one, presenting a challenge for any alternative picture.

Chapter 3 describes what is involved in the procedure of forced expansion. First, I examine the view, which seems to be supported by Frege's writings, that there are no expansions of concepts, only the replacement of one concept by a different one. I claim that this formulation does not capture the whole complexity of non-arbitrary expansions of concepts. Then I present an explication of the phenomenon that makes use of the concept of *truth in a model*, based on adjusting Tarski's definition of truth to our needs. On this basis I distinguish between external expansions, in which elements are added to the realm under discussion, and internal expansions, in which a function is applied to a new realm. Many expansions, both within and outside of mathematics, are of the second type. I also propose a distinction between two types of internal expansion – forced expansions and strongly forced expansions – which I make use of later on. I then present two logics of expansion which were analyzed by Saharon Shelah, who determined that one of them is complete and the other is not.

Chapter 4 discusses the claim that the procedure of expanding functions in accordance with constraints is a fundamental rational process. I begin the chapter with three types of support for this claim. One sort of forced expansion is identical to deduction. Thus, even though expansions and deductions must be distinguished, the procedure of non-arbitrary expansion is a refinement of deduction, in a sense that is explained in the chapter. The procedure of expansion in accordance with constraints can be found in many different areas and on various levels (e.g., sentences, objects, concepts), as is required of a logical operation. I also call attention to the fact that when we ask people to complete partially filled matrices, as is often done in intelligence testing, we are actually asking them to perform a forced expansion. The fact that such tests are generally accepted as a way of revealing people's intellectual capacity shows that we see a connection between forced expansions and rational procedures. On the basis of these types of support I examine the normativity of forced expansions. The chapter ends with an appendix on what makes an expansion fruitful. Even though there is no a priori test for answering this question, I suggest that reflecting on fruitful expansions that have been made in the past, to see what gave them this desirable property, can provide us with general guidelines for evaluating new expansions that suggest themselves to us.

Chapter 5 proposes a picture of the relation between concepts and their expansions that is based on the discussion in the previous chapters. Frege's third argument against the idea of the development of concepts (from chapter 2) can be countered in such a way that his realism and extensionalism are preserved. According to the proposed picture, the range of a concept is not given all at once but is composed of stages that are connected in a treelike structure. The transition from one stage of a concept to another can be formulated as a sentence (whose logic was analyzed in chapter 3). This provides an amendment of Frege's formulations about what happens in the expansion of concepts. Thus it should not be claimed, for example, that Gauss only attempted to grasp the concept of number while Cantor actually did so, as implied by what Frege said on the subject, but rather that Gauss grasped one stage of the concept, thus initiating a link with the concept as a whole, while Cantor, who expanded the concept of number, grasped a more advanced stage. Nevertheless, the picture presented here is an extensionalist one. Instead of attributing a single truth-value to sentences, we attribute a whole tree of truth-values to them – at different stages of concepts the truth-value of sentences containing these concepts is subject to change.

The chapter concludes with a brief discussion of two related issues. When Wittgenstein presented his notion of family resemblance he made use of the phenomenon of the expansion of concepts to obviate the need for a definition (of the word "game"). The idea presented here, however, does not necessitate the abandonment of the notion of definition, even if this is understood as the search for a common essence. Sometimes a definition can be found only as the result of an expansion, since the search for the laws that determine the explication makes it possible to distinguish between the features of the concept and the features that determine the expansion (this issue is discussed further in chapter 7).

The second discussion involves a short description of two attempts to offer a picture of expansions without adhering to Frege's principles. The first suggestion is to abandon the idea of a concept as a tree of stages and to recognize only the stages composing the tree. The second is to soften the distinction between one stage of a concept and the next by claiming that the process occurring within each stage already includes an expansion of the concept. This last suggestion raises the interesting idea that the logical analysis of concepts does not lead to their sets of extensions (as claimed by such thinkers as Quine and Tarski), but rather to seeing them as laws for expanding their extensions in a non-arbitrary way.

Chapter 6 discusses the debate between Frege and the formalists about the ontological status of the products of expansions. In this debate Frege the realist denies the formalists' postulates that "Familiar rules of calculation shall still hold, where possible, for the newly-introduced numbers," and "If no contradiction is anywhere encountered, the introduction of the new numbers is held to be justified" (Frege 1980, sec. 97). The discussion in the previous chapters makes it possible to suggest a compromise here, one that preserves the major intuitions of the debaters. I propose that the rational and negative numbers and the like are produced by expanding the identity relation. In other words, we can set up objects in two stages: first we establish a set of mere formal equations that follow from laws such as the commutative and the associative laws, and then we expand our quantifiers to the new "objects." This raises the following question: if the mathematical objects are obtained from a system given by expansions, where do we start? The answer I propose is that we do not start with the objects at all (not even in the system of natural numbers, as Kronecker postulated when he claimed that they were created by God, while the others were the work of man). We begin with ordinals that do not denote objects, but are themselves obtained as an expansion of the laws of deduction for quantifiers. It seems to me that this provides a method of developing a view of ordinals similar to that of Benacerraf without using the notion of structure, a notion recently proposed in the philosophy of mathematics.

Chapter 7 investigates one of Gödel's arguments – one that attempts to use the process of forced expansion to deduce the independent existence of concepts as well as a capacity to perceive them:

If there is nothing sharp to begin with, it is hard to understand how, in many cases, a vague concept can uniquely determine a sharp one without even the *slightest* freedom of choice (quoted from Wang 1996, p. 233).

I examine the relation between this argument and Gödel's more familiar argument for realism, which relies on the fact that the axioms of set theory are forced on us. After a short comparison with Charles Parsons' (1995) analysis of Gödel's view on perception, I propose an amendment to Gödel's argument for the objective reality of concepts.

Chapter 8 studies the implications that the idea of stretching concepts has for the notion of thought. I shall argue against the idea that a sentence expresses either a complete thought or none at all. Instead, we have to admit a category of inchoate thoughts which correspond to what we grasp before assigning the thought a truth-value by a non-arbitrary expansion. Unlike complete thoughts, inchoate ones are not independent of what would count as a justification of them, and we cannot demand, as Frege does, a sharp dichotomy between judging and grasping them. I end this chapter with a short comparison of my view with that of Wittgenstein on the relation between mathematical theorems and their proofs, which criticizes Frege from a similar angle.

In chapter 9 I apply the results of chapter 8 to the analysis of the philosophical problem posed by the paradoxes of set theory, according to which the paradoxes stem from a careless expansion of concepts and laws. This takes me to an examination of the possible assumptions that lie behind the anxiety reflected in the expression "I was misled by language (reason/intuition)." These, I believe, are the assumptions that there is a clear-cut division between legitimate expressions and meaningless or problematic ones, and that logic cannot start without proposing such a division. Instead, I propose that we divide the expressions of a language into three groups, adding a third category of inchoate expressions. In this view, a paradox is a failed attempt to constitute a space of objects. The illusion here did not result from our incorrectly thinking that a certain expression was meaningful when it was actually meaningless; rather, it resulted from our failure in dealing with inchoate expressions.

I then use this idea to counter Frege's pessimistic reaction to the paradoxes in set theory. I believe that the reason Frege despaired when he received Russell's postcard was due to his requirement that logic cannot operate without ensuring a reference for every proper name. Frege understood that this is an impossible demand, and so he became skeptical of the very possibility of logic. If, however, we adopt the conception of logic developed in this book, according to which logic is involved in the act of constituting the domain of objects, we can propose a different view, one much more hopeful than Frege's reaction to Russell's paradox.

In the current work I am only able to offer the preliminary steps towards a comprehensive study of expansions of concepts. I have confined myself to a logical analysis of this procedure and to its implications on the philosophy of logic. This is, however, a subject that can be delved into much more deeply. In the Epilogue I discuss a number of questions that I am leaving open in this book. I list several kinds of questions that could advance the study of conceptual changes. The most salient ones take the form of whether we should consider a particular domain to be one that was constituted by non-arbitrary expansions. These questions, many of which arose during the course of the book, involve such domains as the space of proofs (or some part of it), the arithmetic of large numbers, etc. Since such questions require special attention, I conclude the book with some methodological remarks about the way they should be dealt with.

Historical background

The history of mathematics and the sciences is replete with examples
of the expansion of concepts. Nowadays we are witness to a growing
interest in the history of mathematics which has given rise to a range
of essays on the history of specific concepts and theories. In this chapter, I should like to concentrate on several turning points and dilemmas
in the development of the idea of expanding concepts and domains.
This will require tracing the emergence of expansions as a general process from specific examples, and distinguishing these developments from
the history of other general and basic notions such as algebraic structures and deduction. At the end of this chapter I briefly survey the
state of the art in the study of expansions in mathematical logic and
philosophy.

EARLY DEBATES

Expansions of concepts began to occur in seventh-century India, with
negative numbers, the irrational numbers, and the zero. In sixteenth-
century Europe a great number of expansions occurred one after another, giving Western mathematics a unique status. The first signs of
this phenomenon were apparently the introduction of the zero and
the beginnings of algebra, which were brought to the West by the
Arabs.

When Western mathematicians developed these ideas, they did not
follow pure logic; in fact, they had to make some compromises on rigor.
If they had not done so, their expansions would have been blocked by
the ancient Greek conception of mathematics, just as this conception
had first blocked the acceptance of the rational numbers and then of the
irrational numbers. The Greek model prevented development in mathematics because it recognized only the natural numbers and required

that all mathematical developments be made according to rigid axioms such as those used in Euclidean geometry.[1]

At first there was great resistance to the negative numbers that were suggested as possible solutions for algebraic equations that apparently had none. Pascal, for example, thought that the very idea of negative numbers was nonsense, since he believed that subtracting any number from a smaller number must yield zero. Arnauld rejected the negative numbers because they violated basic laws that were true for positive numbers. If $a < b$, Arnauld argued, then $a:b$ can never be equal to $b:a$. It is therefore difficult to understand how, for example, $-1:1$ can be equal to $1:-1$.

Similar objections were offered against virtually all developments in modern mathematics.[2] The complex numbers especially were considered total nonsense, and were not accepted until the nineteenth century. Even though we now accept complex numbers as a matter of course, we can still understand these objections.[3] It seems to make no sense to assign a meaning to the square root of a number that cannot have one by definition. Doing so invites analogous questions, such as why we cannot define the immediate successor function on $\frac{1}{2}$ or study vector spaces with negative dimensions. The obvious answer to the first question – that the rational numbers are dense and so there is no meaning to a successor function for them – can no longer be given, since it seems analogous to the argument that we can prove that -1 has no square root. If we could add a whole new set of numbers such that their squares would be negative numbers, then why can we not add new numbers that would be the immediate successors of the fractions?[4]

The numbers that appeared as weird solutions to quadratic equations were variously called "sophistic," "inexplicable," or "impossible." These "nonsensical" numbers, however, proved extremely useful in solving not only problems in mathematics but also problems in physics (e.g., negative velocities and fractions of an hour, etc.). If it were not for the fact that the negative numbers had proved immediately useful, the objections to them could not have been set aside. Eventually it became clear that without this "nonsense" there would be no mathematics – or at least no

---

[1] For example, Cavalieri, a student of Galileo's, consciously decided to abandon the rigid requirements of the ancient Greeks, leaving them to the philosophers.

[2] This point was noticed by Crowe (1992).

[3] An echo of these objections can be seen in students' difficulties in understanding number systems that are expansions of the natural numbers.

[4] A similar question can be found in Frege's argument against the formalists. See chapter 6 below.

modern mathematics. Moreover, without expansions it is hard to see how we could progress in physics. What would our formulas look like if we could not substitute rational numbers for the variables? How would we manage without the idea of negative velocity or vectors? The use of the products of mathematical expansions has increased considerably in modern physics. In the case of the complex numbers, for example, it is hard even to imagine how awkward and unwieldy our formulas would be without them.

The beginning of the attempt to understand complex numbers can be seen in the use of the term "imaginary." This term is a considerable improvement on such words as "nonsensical" or "absurd." Leibniz employed familiar ontological descriptions such as "existing only in the mind," which he also used for relations and anything else that is not an object. This description lies at the heart of his famous saying about imaginary numbers that they are "a fine and wonderful refuge of the divine spirit, almost an amphibian between being and nonbeing" (quoted from Klein 1939, p. 56).

Leibniz suggested the notion of fiction, which helps us describe these peculiar numbers, but the problems they raise are not confined to algebra. The infinitesimals of the new calculus showed that the phenomenon is more general. Mathematicians now had far more power than ever before, but they did not know how to justify this power. While Leibniz's attitude to complex numbers was fairly clear, his attitude to the differentials was much more complicated, as these new entities have a natural interpretation in geometry as the slopes of tangents and in physics as expressions for instantaneous velocity. In this case too Leibniz could not decide if the new entities were fiction or reality.

But since Leibniz did not have a theory of fiction, it was not clear what status could be given to the mathematical entities that had forced themselves upon mathematicians. The differentials and the strange laws obeyed by these peculiar entities were soon subjected to harsh criticism. Berkeley attacked the theory of differentials, calling them "the ghosts of departed quantities." From our present viewpoint, it is hard to find anyone in the history of philosophy who contributed more to the development of rigorous standards in mathematics than Berkeley. More than any other philosopher of his day, he confronted the community of mathematicians and told them that they did not know what they were doing.

Not only were mathematicians unable to solve the problems raised by expansions, but, lacking a theory of mathematical fiction, they apparently could not even formulate clear questions to be answered. According to

Leibniz, for example, only monads exist – not the natural numbers, and not geometric figures. We could say that the square root of −1 is an abstract entity, but in what way is it more abstract than the number 7? For many years philosophers made a distinction between negative numbers, which can be given a fairly simple interpretation, and the square roots of such numbers, which seemed totally absurd, yet they did not have a clear theory according to which the former are only slightly problematic while the latter are seriously so.

Today it is easy for us to say that their problem was that they did not have an interpretation for the complex numbers. But this involves seeing their approach in the light of our modern views, which were accepted only after a paradigm shift. It took time to realize that the problem of the meaning of the complex numbers could be solved by giving an interpretation to all the symbols containing "$\sqrt{-1}$." It is not exactly obvious that we can eliminate the fictional aura of the complex numbers by declaring that the square root of −1 is a point on a plane or identifying it with the ordered pair (0, 1).[5] After all, the mathematicians who use points on a plane as an interpretation of the complex numbers do not actually mean that these numbers really *are* these points, nor does anyone believe that they are merely ordered pairs. These identifications involve conceptual difficulties associated with our basic understanding of what mathematics is.

From product to procedure

Putting aside the ontological status of the products of expansion for the moment, let us examine the actual procedure of expansion. Since fictions are produced by the human faculty of imagination, should we infer that the complex numbers are produced by this faculty? Or, if we do not consider the complex numbers to be fictions, should we say that we discover them? If we do consider them to be fictions, then are they created by the same human faculty that is responsible for creating fictional stories? And if we consider them to be discoveries, then are they discovered in the same way that we discover continents, as Frege said in his argument with the formalists (which we will discuss later)?

This last issue can be sharpened by an examination of early debates about the way to expand functions. These debates differed from those

---

[5] F. J. Servois (1785–1864) criticized the geometric interpretation of complex numbers as being a geometrical mask applied to algebraic forms; the direct use of them seemed to him simple and more efficient.

about the differential calculus and the status of complex numbers in that they did not involve the acceptance of strange new objects that we have every reason to believe cannot possibly exist. Rather, the debates about the expansion of functions required changing the definitions of some of our concepts. This distinction led to another one. Although at that time no one had ever thought of the possibility of expanding the *number system* in different ways, it was well known that *functions* can be expanded in different ways. In each such case it was therefore necessary to determine the best way of expanding the function. No one asked whether a particular expansion of a function was a fiction or a discovery; mathematicians simply tried to find the best possible expansion. Indeed, the very existence of the stormy debates about which expansion is the best shows that the expansions of functions were not regarded as fictions.

This point can be sharpened even further. The best-known debate of this sort was undoubtedly the one between Johann Bernoulli and Leibniz on the way to expand $\log(-1)$. As this debate is important for the entire issue of expansions, it is worth discussing it in detail. Bernoulli claimed that:

$$\log x = \int \frac{\mathrm{d}x}{x} = \int \frac{\mathrm{d}(-x)}{-x} = \log(-x).$$

From this he deduced the equation

$$\log x = \log(-x)$$

and therefore

$$\log(-1) = \log 1 = 0.$$

Another proof could be brought for this claim. If we denote $\log(-1)$ by x we get

$$0 = x + x,$$

since

$$0 = \log(1) = \log[(-1) \times (-1)] = \log(-1) + \log(-1).$$

Therefore

$$\log(-1) = 0.$$

Leibniz opposed this definition, claiming that the axiom involving differentials that Bernoulli was trying to use for expanding the logarithm function is not valid for the logarithms of negative numbers. One of the arguments he presented in his lengthy correspondence with Bernoulli is the following. If $\log(-1)$ were 0 or any other real number, then the logarithm of the square root of -1 would also be 0, since the logarithm of the square root of a number is always half the logarithm of the number itself, and half of 0 is 0. This result seemed absurd to Leibniz, but he nevertheless took the trouble to point out additional problems with Bernoulli's expansion.[6]

This problem was decided by Euler who, in his own words, was "tortured" by the "paradoxes" that he had to face in his attempt to discover the right answer. Euler "guessed" it from taking into consideration the analytical properties of the power and the sine and cosine functions. He ended up with the following definition:

$$\log(-1) = \pi i + 2k\pi \quad \text{for } k = 1, 2, 3 \ldots$$

See Kline (1972, vol. II, pp. 406–11) for a short description of the debate.

This debate, unlike the one about fiction, was based on the use of reason. The question of what $\log(-1)$ should be was a real problem that bothered mathematicians for a long time. They did not treat the question as similar to "What is the logarithm of the moon?" Both Bernoulli and Euler believed that there was a true value of $\log(-1)$, even though they did not know what it was, and even though, from our viewpoint, they had no idea what sort of number it should be or even if such a number could be defined. Even if they may have seen themselves as dealing with fictions, they attacked the problem just as if it were completely realistic.

Now although the arguments used in this debate appealed to reason, they were not based on strict logic. Indeed, as is the case with all functions, the expansion of the logarithm cannot be deduced from the original definition of a logarithm. In general, the mathematicians had a *tentative* definition of the function, but when they looked for an expansion they were actually going counter to this definition. Just as the mathematical objects we add are in a no man's land between the real and the imaginary, so the arguments we use in expanding functions lie somewhere between deductions and analogies.

---

[6] The reason why it seemed absurd to him was never specified – I can only speculate that it had to do with his requirement that every function must be one-to-one. Compare this with my remarks in the appendix to chapter 4.

Leibniz attempted to prove that $\log(-1)$ is nonsense by substituting $x = (-2)$ in

$$\log(1 + x) = x - \frac{x}{2} + \frac{x}{3} + \cdots$$

which yields:

$$\log(-1) = -2 - \frac{4}{2} - \frac{8}{3} - \cdots$$

We can better understand the procedure of expanding functions if we ask ourselves whether other rational beings with the same arithmetic that we have would also have formulated their higher mathematics in the same way. Let us say that we manage to send a spaceship to a planet of Alpha Centauri and we discover that its inhabitants use arithmetic. Does this give us reason to predict that if we return there a thousand years later we will find them using negative numbers, perhaps even complex numbers? And if we find that they use the power function, is it also probable that they will expand it to the zero? It seems that there is some basis for believing that we will find all these developments.

This idea is sharpened through the following radical example. Suppose we were to remove the 7 from the set of natural numbers. Although we can easily describe such an operation, we clearly feel a resistance to considering the remaining set legitimate. We want to say that if some tribe had an arithmetic that forbade adding 7 to any other number, someday a member of that tribe would rebel and begin adding 7s. Moreover, if some community had an operation that was close to our own addition but not exactly the same, our intuition is that they would eventually come to use the same addition operation that we do. We feel that this is a natural process and we sense its power when we consider the unnatural situation of this hypothetical tribe.

This special power of the way we formulate and expand mathematical operations makes it sensible to call such expansions "forced expansions of concepts." Using this expression enables us to avoid the dilemma of whether discovery or fiction is involved here, as well as the use of terms such as "deduction" or "analogy." But at this stage we do not understand the nature of this process; we have merely found a name for it.

PEACOCK'S FORGOTTEN PLANE

The first steps in treating the issue of expansions that are not merely comments about some particular expansion can be found only after Euler. One example is that of the late eighteenth-century philosopher Solomon Maimon. Maimon distinguishes between types of cognition. He adds what he calls symbolic cognition to Kant's a priori and empirical cognition:

In order to overcome this difficulty we need symbolic cognition, that is, first we substitute symbols for the things to be symbolized and then we replace each symbol by another symbol of equal force, and so on. In this way each new formula creates a new truth. It is thus possible to discover truths, however hidden they may be, without much effort, even mechanically. But this creates a new difficulty, namely, sometimes we obtain symbolic combinations or formulas that have no real existence, that is, that do not denote any real object, such as imaginary numbers, tangents or the cosine of a straight angle . . . Although mathematics gains much from the new analysis . . . mathematicians who are not sufficiently careful encounter difficulties that were unknown to their predecessors (Maimon [1790] 1965, vol. II, p. 412).

In this passage Maimon describes a general problem, claiming that the differentials, the complex numbers, and expansions of functions are all part of the same topic. We begin with a set of symbols that have a denotation, but when the formalism is left to itself, it can be said to create symbols by following analogical constructions that yield nonsense. The Leibnizian trust in symbolization is therefore in need of a critique.

Maimon was perhaps the first to link the problem of meaningless symbols with other philosophical problems. For him, most philosophical problems are associated with the nature of language. Moreover, he rejects Kant's argument in the first *Critique*, in the second part of the first antinomy, where Kant argues against the finitude of the world on the assumption that "a beginning is an existence which is preceded by a time in which the thing does not exist" (Kant 1933, B-455). Maimon replies that if the world has a beginning then the expression "before the universe began" is like "the square root of -1" (Maimon [1794] 1965, vol. V, p. 241), and this, he thought, entails that Kant's argument is not valid.[7] I will also follow Maimon's direction, but only in chapter 9, after I develop the notion of inchoate thought in chapter 8.

Maimon had a well-developed theory of fiction, which was admired by the neo-Kantian Veihinger. He sees mathematical fictions involving the symbolic kind of knowledge as primary, and analyses metaphysical fiction in accordance with his analysis of the mathematical sort. Moreover, he is even willing to claim that metaphysical issues can be discussed through useful fictions the way mathematicians talk about "cos 0."

One important attempt to deal with the problems raised by expansions was that of the nineteenth-century mathematician George Peacock, which was developed in response to Berkeley's criticism. Peacock distinguished between arithmetical and symbolical algebra. The former deals only with positive quantities, and therefore does not permit

---

[7] Ironically, Stephen Hawking and James Hartle have recently proposed a theory which allows time to be imaginary. At the end of my argument I too come to a similar conclusion, but for this we will have to wait for chapter 9.

the subtraction of a number from a smaller number, or any operations or expressions that might produce complex numbers. Peacock considered arithmetical algebra to be a logically complete system, but he claimed it was not sufficient to capture the developments that had occurred in algebra since Vieta. Symbolical algebra, in contrast, ignores the requirement that symbols should stand for positive quantities, thus permitting any number to be represented. Symbols are abstract because of the necessity of representing something, although it might be possible to give them an interpretation later on. Peacock was the first to begin investigating the idea of a formal calculus in a fairly clear way:

> So that it may thus become essentially a science of symbols and their combinations, constructed upon its own rules, which may be applied to arithmetic and to all other sciences by interpretation: by this means, interpretation will *follow*, and not *precede*, the operations of algebra and their results (Peacock 1834, pp. 194–5).

We must avoid trying to understand Peacock's idea in present-day terms, as if it were a formal syntactic investigation into the world of symbols. The modern concepts of logic and algebra tempt us to understand Peacock that way, and this may be the reason that historians see Peacock's view as the beginning of the concept of algebraic structure, which would later be generalized in Tarski's concept of a model. Peacock explains that symbolical algebra is not obtained from arithmetical algebra by deduction; what is most important for our present purposes, however, is Peacock's statement that the laws that are valid for algebraic research are *suggested* by arithmetical algebras. He presents the following formulation of the "principle of the permanence of equivalent forms":

> Whatever form is algebraically equivalent to another when expressed in general symbols, *must continue* to be equivalent, whatever those symbols denote.
> Whatever equivalent form is discoverable in arithmetical algebra considered as *the science of suggestion*, when the symbols are general in their form, though specific in their value, will continue to be an equivalent form when the symbols are general in their nature as well as in their form (Peacock 1834, pp. 198–9; my emphasis).

The question that interests us here is how to understand Peacock's "must continue." We have already mentioned his claim that it is not a matter of deduction, since symbolic algebra is independent of arithmetic. It is also known that Peacock did not accept Euler's view that these laws are *always* valid for new cases. Still, we cannot infer that Peacock thought that arithmetic is only the motivation for the laws of algebra in the sense that these laws were abstracted from arithmetic and we are investigating them separately.

The laws that are obtained through Peacock's principle are not seen as empty formal laws but as *suggested* by arithmetical algebra, which is limited to the study of the positive numbers. This type of suggestion does not abrogate the autonomy of symbolical algebra, but it does require us to maintain the validity of all the laws we discovered in arithmetical algebra and extend them to the new cases as well. Peacock does not accept the claim that the motivation for the commutative law is the fact that the natural numbers obey it and we want to abstract and study this concept, the way we study the axioms of groups. Many textbooks justify mathematicians' interest in groups by the fact that there are many models that can be interpreted as obeying the axioms of groups. In Peacock's view, however, the commutative law has to be true of all numbers. This view can explain Hamilton's great difficulty years later in accepting the possibility of numbers that do not obey the commutative law. Hamilton tried to force this law on the new system that he developed for fifteen years before he could accept the necessity for abandoning it. If it had merely been a formal law, it would be very hard to explain Hamilton's insistence on trying to keep it in his new number system of quaternions.

Peacock's principle is an attempt to deal systematically with the phenomenon of expansions, but it is clearly insufficient. As can be seen from the example of Hamilton, it is not sensitive to the fact that some laws must be abandoned at times, since laws that are valid for arithmetic are not necessarily always valid outside of arithmetic. This does not mean, however, that we have to ignore all of Peacock's suggestions, some of which may be useful for our purposes.

Another problem with Peacock's principle is that it involves only a particular transition from arithmetic to algebra, but does not attempt to generalize to all the transitions from one system to another system that are suggested by it. Finally, and no less important, Peacock is not even aware of the possibility of analyzing the transition from one system to the other by formal devices.

The next development in the field of expansions was due to Duncan Gregory, in the first half of the nineteenth century, who came out against the idea that the laws extracted from the case of arithmetic have normative value. Gregory saw the laws abstracted from a mathematical structure as axioms that could be interpreted as applying to any class of objects, just as the axioms of groups can be interpreted as applying to numbers, rotations of geometric objects, and the like. Boole, who was familiar with Gregory's work, applied his ideas to logic as well. He discovered a new interpretation of the laws of addition and multiplication as being applicable to what we now call disjunction and conjunction. Boole showed how the logical relations between propositions could be written in the form of algebraic equations. He thus treated the laws of logic as if they were the laws of some arithmetical structure.

A later version of Peacock's principle was formulated by Hankel (1867), but the two versions were separated by the vast developments that had taken place in all branches of mathematics, including the very meaning of mathematics itself, during the course of the nineteenth century. Some of these developments were Hamilton's provision of a basis for the complex numbers by identifying them with ordered pairs of real numbers, the discovery of various geometries, Cauchy's first attempts at providing a basis for the differential calculus, and the vast extension of our knowledge of algebra. The beautiful days of Euler were over and mathematicians had learned that there was no contradiction between the standards set by the Greeks and fruitful, useful mathematics. It was this attempt to adhere to standards that led to an even stronger demand for rigorous proofs than that of the Greeks, as can be seen in Hilbert's work on the foundations of geometry towards the end of nineteenth century, Dedekind's provision of a basis for the real numbers and the natural numbers, and Peano's and Frege's attempts to understand the concept of a proof.

As far as I know, Peano was the first mathematician after Peacock to discuss the phenomenon of expansions in mathematics. He represented an improvement over Peacock in that he understood the importance of the process of expansion for the formalization of mathematics in general. Peano worked, in parallel with Frege, on creating a logical notation for presenting mathematical proofs; in one of his letters to Frege he expressed the idea that a notation must be structured in such a way as to include the possibility of expanding mathematical functions (quoted in Frege 1977a, vol. II, footnote to sec. 58; I shall return to this issue in chapter 5). The symbols denoting functions would always be open to the possibility of further expansions, while the symbols denoting objects would be closed. As we shall see, in this view even the identity sign is not unambiguous, but must be seen as capable of development. This attempt of Peano's did not actually result in a clear formalism that describes the dynamics of such development; even Peano's system for writing proofs was not accepted by the community of logicians, who preferred Frege's system. Frege was aware of Peano's project when he expressed his opposition to the whole idea of expansions, and it may be this very awareness that made his opposition so strong.

THE CURRENT STATE

At the present time, all the mathematical objects that had previously been called "nonsense," or "fictions," as well as Leibniz's amphibious creatures, can all be placed within a space of unproblematic objects. Moreover, thanks to Gödel's completeness theorem, we know that if there is an object for a first-order theory, and this theory is consistent, then there must be a model for this theory that is made up of sets. At the present time there are no number-words or other mathematical expressions that supposedly have no reference, and mathematicians today appear certain that they will be able to find some reference for any symbol that crops up in the future.

Moreover, not only the products of expansion but also the procedure itself has been discussed from time to time. Robinson's notion of model completeness, Cohen's notion of forcing and van Frassen's (1966) concept of supervaluation can all be viewed as echoes of Peacock's principle of the permanence of forms. In fact, even Hilbert's program of viewing the relation between talk about infinity and talk about finite domains as similar to the relation between the complex numbers and the real ones is an echo of Peacock's principle. Mathematical logic thus supplies a set of different notions of expansion. However, such expansions stem from mathematical rather than philosophical interests.[8]

In modern philosophy we constantly find new types of expansions of concepts and principles. Brouwer's argument against classical logic is that its acceptance of the law of the excluded middle is the result of an intuitive expansion of a logic which is valid in the finite case. He insists, however, that a more careful study of mathematical objects will show that the laws of classical logic are not valid for infinite totalities. (This shows that Brouwer is assuming that he himself is not expanding the logic of finite aggregates in a different way from that of the classical logicians, but rather uncovering the correct laws of such aggregates, an assumption which obviously needs to be thoroughly examined.)

---

[8] Robinson's interest in model completeness derives from his desire to contribute to the "metamathematics of algebra" (Robinson 1955, preface). Cohen's notion of forcing concerns the theory of sets and questions of the independence of axioms, and is less about philosophical or logical issues.

Expansions are connected with intuitionism in Hilbert's view as well. Hilbert admitted that we expand those axioms of classical logic that were found to be correct in the case of finitistic mathematics, but he considered this expansion a legitimate one. Just as the commutative law, which was valid for the natural numbers, could be expanded to the complex numbers as well, so the law of the excluded middle could be expanded from finitary statements of intuitive number theory to ideal statements that apparently refer to infinite totalities. Hilbert considered this analogy to be a way of establishing the certitude of classical mathematics. (He did not, however, even consider the possibility of expanding the laws of classical logic differently, so as to arrive at a logic incompatible with the classical one.)

Another thesis that makes use of the idea of expansions can be found in the analysis of antinomies in philosophy and the attempt to understand the paradoxes of set theory. This thesis, which, as we shall see in chapter 9, was adopted by the most important twentieth-century logicians, asserts that paradoxes are the result of the incautious expansion of our concepts.[9] Kant's analysis, which I presented in the Preface, claims that every concept has a clear range of applicability, and stretching it beyond this range leads to antinomies. Thus antinomies are seen as a sign that a concept has been stretched too far. Russell's theory of types is a Kantian move with the aim of avoiding paradoxes.

Another philosophical discussion which raises the issue of developments of concepts is in the attempt to understand the nature of scientific revolutions and the conceptual changes they involve. Such conceptual changes are more than changes in the extension of concepts. Nevertheless, there is an analogy between these conceptual changes and the ones we are discussing here. This analogy involves a variety of issues – e.g., the question whether the theory of relativity has changed our concept of space to the point that it is incommensurable with Newton's concepts is analogous to the question of whether Cantor's concept of number is a conceptual shift from Gauss's notion. A more subtle connection has to do with Putnam's discussion of the possibility of changing the laws of logic due to empirical findings. Putnam (1975a, 1994) claims that Einstein's scientific revolution, which has been empirically confirmed, did not change our geometrical concepts, although it contains results

---

[9] Sometimes this thesis is presented as a way of resolving the paradoxes. This is how I read Kripke's criticism of Tarski. Kripke claims that the concept of truth should be seen not as belonging to a meta-language, but as a predicate that is not defined on all sentences, so that there are some sentences, such as the liar sentence, to which the truth predicate cannot be expanded.

that we could not understand before Einstein. In the same way, it is possible that a physical theory will force us to abandon certain logical truths. In such cases, an example of which Putnam believes to have occurred in quantum mechanics, the change in logic should not be interpreted as a change in the meaning of the logical operators, but rather as the refutation of a logical principle. The controversy about this issue, which has been going on since the 1970s, involves problems in the philosophy of language which I touch upon briefly later in this book (in chapters 5 and 8).

Mark Steiner (1998) recently used the idea of forced expansions to suggest a new formulation of the issue of the applicability of mathematics to physics. He asks how concepts obtained through non-arbitrary expansions, determined by pure mathematical considerations, can find natural applications in physics. Steiner presents examples of cases where people attempted unsuccessfully to apply a concept to a physical system, and then found that a forced expansion would enable the concept to fit the system better. This provides Steiner with an argument against naturalism in science.

Another application of expansions can be found in Manders (1989). Manders criticizes the discussion of ontology in mathematics for being too closely tied to physics. He proposes that mathematical objects emerge out of internal mathematical considerations, in order to simplify our study of the original systems. Manders offers a formal criterion for distinguishing a fruitful expansion from a useless one, and recommends examining its implications for epistemology.

Expansions and other changes of concepts are also associated with important issues in Wittgenstein's work. Perhaps the most important are the notion of family resemblance and the idea that a proof in mathematics changes the concepts involved in it and determines the meaning of the conclusion, both of which are discussed in detail below. Wittgenstein also presents a methodological recommendation to compare changes in language with changes in mathematics (1958, no. 23). He says this explicitly as well:

What does a man do when he constructs (invents) a new language; on what principle does he operate? For this principle is the concept of "language." Does every newly constructed language broaden (alter) the concept of language? – Consider its relationship to the earlier concept: that depends on how the earlier concept was established. – Think of the relation of complex numbers to the earlier concept of number; and again of the relation of a *new* multiplication to the general concept of the multiplication of cardinal numbers, when two particular (perhaps very large) cardinal numbers are written down for the first time and multiplied together (Wittgenstein 1974, p. 115).

This remark of Wittgenstein's suggests seeing computations involving large numbers as the result of an expansion. This suggestion, which needs to be examined carefully, raises some general questions. When can a given area be seen as one that is constituted by expansions of concepts? Can such a position be held for empirical claims as well? Can logical deduction be considered a type of non-arbitrary expansion? In general, what would count as an answer to a question of this sort?

Whatever the answer to such questions, Wittgenstein is clearly saying that the expansions that occur in modern mathematics are not solely an issue for mathematics, but should be discussed in a wider setting. I take this as a strong recommendation to tie certain developments in mathematical logic to basic philosophical questions.

I could cite even more examples of topics where the issue of expansions arises, but it is not my intention to present a list of all the occurrences of this issue in modern philosophy. I have chosen the most prominent examples – the ones that show that this is not a procedure that is confined to mathematics – with the hope that the reader will keep them in mind while reading the rest of this book.

In summary, the products of expansions, such as the complex numbers, lie between fiction and reality, while the procedure of expansion falls somewhere between deductions and analogies. Peacock went a step further when he spoke about suggestions. But the story is actually rather more complicated, as we shall see in the following chapters.

CHAPTER 2

Frege's opposition

As we saw in the Introduction, Frege summarily dismissed any notion of conceptual expansions. Since his theory is the simplest and the strongest, it will be useful to begin with it. There is another reason for beginning with Frege's position. Even though Frege started out by questioning the nature of numbers and attempting to understand deduction, he was the first to do so on the basis of a broader view of language, thought, and reference. In this respect no logician prior to Frege was better able to provide a philosophical dimension to the issue of expansions, which can be useful for the philosophy of language. Thus, examining Frege's opposition to expansions should be a natural way of getting into the philosophical discussions of expansions, some of which were mentioned in the previous chapter.

Frege presents three arguments to demonstrate that the idea of the expansion of concepts is incoherent. These arguments can be separated from Frege's inner motivations for abolishing the idea,[1] and therefore deserve careful study. I present them in order of importance, beginning with the least important.

THE ARGUMENT FROM REALISM

Frege's realism about concepts and their place in the world of reference leads naturally to the notion that concepts cannot change, and thus cannot be expanded. Once concepts are detached from the thinking subject, they do not undergo the developments that subjects do. This idea is grounded in the intuition that a change in our knowledge involves a change in ourselves rather than in the concepts dealt with. When, for

---

[1] The best example of this sort of motivation is his definition of a number as a set of equinumerous concepts. If we allow concepts to expand it may not be possible to decide unambiguously whether to add or subtract a concept to or from the extension of a particular number. The arguments I present here are not biased in this respect.

example, we say that a child has developed to the point where she can grasp the concept of energy, we do not mean that such learning involves a change in this concept; rather, the child's development, in which she becomes a person who grasps the concept of energy, does not affect the concept itself at all. The idea that a consideration of this sort is what led Frege to reject the notion of conceptual development is supported by the following passage:

For the logical concept there is no development, no history . . . If instead of this sort of talk one said "history of the attempt to grasp a concept" or "history of the grasp of a concept," it would seem to me far more appropriate: for the concept is something objective that we do not form and is not formed in us, but that we try to grasp and finally, it is hoped, really grasp – if we have not mistakenly sought something where there is nothing ("The Law of Inertia," in Frege 1984, p. 113).

The notion of the objectivity of concepts and truth was intended to refute the evolutionary notions of truth that flourished in the nineteenth century. The idea is that truth does not develop as human beings do. It may even seem that in order for the notion of human development to be conceivable we must assume that truth and thought are objective and that time does not affect them.

In this section I examine the intuition that children do not alter the concepts they acquire as they learn them. Frege's realism with regard to concepts provides a way of anchoring the intuition that when children acquire the concept of energy, for example, they do not develop the concept but only discover it. I will therefore try to see whether concept realism actually makes it possible to avoid the possibility of concept changes. It is possible, however, to try to explain the intuition that children do not change concepts in the process of acquiring them even without assuming that concepts exist in a Platonic realm. One such explanation would involve seeing concepts as immanent in a community. We would therefore say that children acquire concepts rather than form them because they have to learn to use the concepts the way they are used in their community. This suggestion is analyzed later in this section.

The attempt to use realism to construct a strong argument against the possibility that concepts can develop is not a simple matter. It is not at all clear how to deduce that concepts cannot develop from the claim that they exist in an objective world. Frege belongs to the tradition

that "concepts are not in the head" – that we grasp concepts the way
we perceive objects.[2] But it is precisely this comparison that raises the
following simple question: since the objectivity of objects (say, horses)
does not prevent them from changing and developing, why should the
objectivity of concepts prevent them from developing? Thus, even if we
agree that the concept of 7 does not change, this fact cannot be deduced
from the assumption that this concept is an entity independent of the
human mind.[3] The argument from realism to refute the possibility of
change does not distinguish between concepts and empirical objects.
Since the latter clearly do undergo changes, this is a major problem for
Frege's argument.

There are at least two different ways of demonstrating that the idea
of the objectivity of concepts contradicts the idea that concepts can
develop. One way is to assume a Platonic ontology and to argue that since
there are no changes or developments in the Platonic realm, concepts
cannot change. In order to establish this argument it is necessary to
provide metaphysical considerations to show that there cannot be any
changes in the world of ideas. Without such considerations the Platonic
realm would seem to be unchanging by its very definition, and so it
cannot be used to show the impossibility of change in a non-circular
manner.

The other version seems to me to fit the spirit of Frege's philosophy
better, as I understand it. I see Frege as saying that concepts do not change
because what they are derived from – namely, thoughts – do not undergo
changes.[4] Frege repeatedly insists that the content I grasp when I understand the Pythagorean theorem is the same content that was grasped
by Pythagoras – that the thought of this theorem has not undergone
any changes. In general, human culture, like human science, would not
be possible if knowledge and beliefs could not be transmitted from one
era to the next. Now, if the thoughts are the same, then the concepts –
which are presumably derived from an analysis of the thoughts – cannot
be different. Since this is consistent with Frege's admission that he began
with thoughts and then arrived at concepts, it would seem that there is
no change or development in the space of concepts because there is no
way of understanding the notion of a change in thoughts.

---

[2] The idea that concepts "are not in the head" is not meant only to imply that one's internal state
does not determine what one is thinking about, but is used in the ordinary sense in which we say
that chairs "are not in the head."

[3] Frege believes that even though 7 is different from Julius Caesar, it is not a different sort of object
from Caesar.

[4] This dependence is not necessarily ontological, as Frege can be interpreted as claiming that
without concepts there are no real thoughts.

It is doubtful whether an argument of this sort will suffice for our purposes. After all, if the concepts that are derived from the analysis of thoughts cannot change, then why are the objects that are derived from the same thoughts nevertheless capable of changing? This is merely a variant of the previous question: what is it about change that makes objects but not concepts vulnerable to it? Aristotle's metaphysics answers this question by postulating that form does not change, because it is responsible for change, while substance is defined as that which can undergo changes.[5] The non-metaphysical argument that attempts to deduce the unchangeability of concepts from that of thoughts thus requires a metaphysical complement which Frege does not supply.

Even the notion that thoughts do not change, however, cannot be derived from a direct analysis of their ontological status, but only from constraints that are imposed on the concept of communication. If it were not for this we could question Frege's certainty that the thought grasped by Pythagoras is indeed the same thought that he himself grasped. Do I know that I am grasping the same thought because I have placed my thought beside his and have convinced myself that the two are the same? Alternatively, if Pythagoras' thought has indeed changed, then his original thought is no longer graspable, and I have nothing but my own thought! Frege has no direct argument showing that we grasp the same thought. This lack may tell us something about the sense in which Frege grasped the unchangeability of thoughts, which is connected with the fact that he did not adopt a metaphysical defense of the unchangeability of concepts. It is not because thoughts exist in a third world that we believe they are unchanging. Rather, it is the intersubjectivity of language, which is a condition for communication, that guarantees the unchangeability of thoughts, and it is the latter that impels us to locate them in a third world.[6]

Let us sum up the discussion so far. We began with the intuition that children do not alter the concepts they acquire, and the attempt to use realism to anchor this view. But then difficulties arose. We could

---

[5] This postulate suggests, as least as an amusing notion, the opposite postulate: that it is the conceptual part that changes in time, while the objects are unchanging substances. Then the conflict between the two alternative postulates is tantamount to the question of why we prefer the statement "Jack was fat last year, but now he has changed and is thin, although the concept of fatness has not changed" to the statement "Jack has remained the same, but the concept of fatness has changed so that it is no longer true that Jack is fat."

[6] There is another no less problematic objection: even if thoughts do not change, it is possible that a concept derived by decomposing a thought undergoes a change which leaves the thought intact. This notion requires two different conceptual decompositions of the same thought, which leads us to other principles of Frege's that cannot be discussed here. It is a doubt of this sort that leads to the third argument, presented below.

not explain why the assumption that concepts exist outside the subject should entail that they cannot change. We then tried to explain the unchanging nature of concepts through the assumption that thoughts do not change, and ended up with the argument – although it is not strictly deductive – that the idea that thoughts do not change is a precondition of the intersubjectivity of communication, not a stipulation of a third world of inert thoughts. But this takes us away from the Fregean realism we began with, as we have made thoughts, and therefore concepts as well, immanent to the community. If that is the case then we must now explain why concepts that are immanent in a community cannot change as the community itself changes.

Even if it is true, as I have been claiming, that children do not develop concepts such as that of energy, but rather learn to grasp them, this intuition is not sufficient for attaining the conclusion that Frege is striving for. The process in which children learn a concept of energy in use among a community of speakers is not exactly analogous with the changes in language and concepts that can occur within that community. Because of the difference between the two, we can understand the development of the child's conception as an entry into the community of speakers without needing to claim that concepts have an independent existence that cannot undergo changes. As soon as we speak of a community we make reference to a rich structure of conventions, forms of life, and rules of behavior – which do not exist in the case of the child. Indeed, at the same time that we say that children acquire language, we also say that the English language itself has changed when we speak about the differences between Old English and Modern English.

In order to distinguish the community, and not only the individual, from the concept, it is not enough to make use of the idea that the child acquires concepts rather than developing them. It is necessary to see the relation between the community and the concept as similar to that between the community and an independent physical object like the sun, or between the community's knowledge and the truth. The idea of the attempt to grasp something is generally familiar when the thing to be grasped is an object or the truth-value of a proposition, but not when it is a concept. Distinguishing the community from the concept is not the same sort of thing as distinguishing it from the truth. When we link a language to a community, we are not committing ourselves to the claim that objective truth is also in the community's possession. There is a great gap between the intuitive claim that there are *truths* that the community does not now possess but that it will be able to grasp someday, and the claim that certain *concepts* are not grasped by the community, because the community grasps the concepts even when it accepts a false proposition containing these concepts.[7]

Thus, even if we accept the idea that children acquire concepts rather than developing them, we still see no reason not to claim that the community in which they live does shape and alter concepts. Frege's first argument, and the metaphysical ideas about the status of concepts that we analyzed above, do not help us here. The problem is that Frege's formulation conflicts with the conclusion we reached in the previous section. If it turns out that the reason he gives for the claim that concepts do not change is not that they exist in an unchanging Platonic realm but rather that thoughts are fixed because communication is intersubjective, then it is hard to disconnect concepts from the community. The conflict exists because on the one hand we claim that language resides in the community and at the same time we allow concepts to transcend the community that fails to grasp them.

The problem with Frege's formulation involves the very expression "the attempt to grasp a concept." How can I know if I have really grasped a concept, and I am not merely "attempting" to grasp it? With what sort of thing am I in contact when I attempt to grasp a concept but do not really do so? Did Gauss only attempt to grasp the concept of number, while Cantor "really" grasped it after he expanded it? If so, would we say that what Gauss had was only a subjective sense of the concept, which, as such, has no connection with the objective concept of number? The question becomes even sharper when we recall that, in Frege's view, if a term does not denote anything, then, if it has a sense at all, this sense belongs to fiction rather than to science. Thus an expression that does not denote a whole concept is no different from "Hamlet," and so Gauss and his colleagues were working in some imaginary world rather than in mathematics. These and similar arguments demonstrate that Frege's formulation is an avoidance of the problem rather than a serious attempt to describe what is actually going on.[8]

---

[7] Holding this position for forced expansions would entail that, as long as the concept of temperature has not been expanded to apply to black holes, the community has not yet grasped the concept of temperature, and this seems extremely odd to me.

[8] Later on Frege changed his description of what happens when concepts seem to undergo changes. Instead of talking about unsuccessful attempts to grasp concepts, he said that there were two different concepts, one of which included the other, but neither of which undergoes any change. The discussion of the third argument also leads naturally to this conclusion. I return to the problems involved in this description at the beginning of chapter 5.

FULL DETERMINACY OF CONCEPTS

Another argument against the idea of expansion of concepts involves Frege's recurrent demand, in all of his writings, that every concept be defined everywhere. The expansion of a concept means that a concept that was not defined on a certain object will now be defined on it, but this itself, in Frege's view, demonstrates that what existed before the expansion was not actually a concept.

In contrast to the previous argument, in the present one the conclusion follows immediately from the premise. The question it provokes is what basis there can be for Frege's premise that concepts which are not defined everywhere are not actually concepts. If this premise is accepted, then the expression "a concept which is true or false of only some of the things in the world" becomes contradictory. A better way to put this is that when there is an expression with the form of a predicate, but it is not defined on some of the objects in the world, then this expression does not denote any concept. However, this requirement of Frege's is strange, as the undefined state under consideration does not involve vagueness.

When vagueness is at stake, with all the paradoxes associated with it, we can understand why logic must avoid it. We can understand that logic requires that every concept have sharp boundaries, and that it considers boundaries that are not sharp as no boundaries at all. But it is possible to keep the metaphor of sharp boundaries yet allow undefined states: one can unambiguously determine when a predicate is true, when it is false, and when it is undefined. All that is needed is to agree that the predicate divides the domain of objects into three parts rather than only two.

Frege does distinguish between these two situations. The first sort, in which a concept is not defined everywhere, can be eliminated by an arbitrary assignment of values of the predicate on the rest of the domain. Nevertheless, it is not clear why Frege is opposed to concepts that are not defined everywhere. There is an obvious difference between a name that does not denote anything and a predicate whose truth-value is not defined for every object. As Dummett explains (1973, p. 170), when a name does not refer to anything, we are justified in claiming that the whole sentence is without a truth-value, but in the case of predicates that are defined on only part of their domain we do say that the predicates are true of some of the objects. An example will make this clearer. For Frege, the fact that we cannot add Clinton to 7 is evidence that the term "+" does not denote a function and that the ordinary expression "$2 + 7 = 9$" belongs to fiction. Without an explanation for this ban, we

cannot understand Frege's opposition to expansions as derived from the
second argument.[9]

Frege's suggestion that every partially defined concept should be arbitrarily completed so as to become a fully defined concept conflicts
with mathematical practice, which accepts functions that are not defined
everywhere and deliberately avoids defining them arbitrarily (as in the
case of dividing by 0[10]). There is a whole mathematical area of research
on complex functions, called analytical continuation, which deals with
the expansions of analytic functions to new domains, and so can only
work with functions that are not yet defined everywhere. The case of partially defined recursive function is another example. As in the previous
argument, the connections between Frege's realism and this requirement
of his are not clear: how can it be that if one object is removed from the
domain of definition of a concept, then the concept ceases to exist in the
Platonic world?[11] In fact, Frege's very willingness to accept an arbitrary
completion of the definition of a concept demonstrates that he does not
take the objective existence of concepts seriously. But this is not the point
I want to discuss here.

Dummett claims that Frege cannot accept predicates defined on only
part of the domain. He suggests describing partially defined predicates as
a situation stemming from the fact "that we have not completely specified
the reference of the predicate." But then he adds that Frege would ask,
"Does it have a reference or doesn't it?" (1973, p. 170) and that the answer
that the predicate is incompletely specified would be "distasteful" to him.
Dummett argues further that a predicate which is not defined everywhere
actually "denotes" the set of concepts obtained by completing it and thus
does not denote anything at all. Just as a proper name must refer to only
one thing, every predicate must also refer to a single concept.

Before responding to this claim of Dummett's I would like to consider Cora Diamond's explanation of Frege's position, which goes much
further than Dummett's on this point. She claims that Frege's avoidance of concepts that are not defined everywhere is linked to two issues.
One is that incompletely defined predicates would abolish logic as a systematic science, and the other is that Frege's paradigm of decomposing

---

[9] Later on in the same book (1973, p. 646), Dummett criticizes Frege's hostility to partially defined
concepts and suggests using a many-sorted logic to avoid the problem.

[10] When mathematicians deal with stereographic projections in complex function theory, a number
divided by 0 is defined as infinity, but this is not an arbitrary definition.

[11] Gödel, for example, believed in the objective existence of concepts – and, as we shall see, in an
even stronger sense than Frege – but he permitted concepts to be partially undefined as long as
the boundaries between the defined and the undefined parts are clear.

the sense of sentences in science, which is connected with his principle of compositionality, would also be eliminated. Diamond's discussion of these issues leads us away from the relatively dry issue of whether logic is possible for partially defined concepts, toward the basic principles of Frege's view, including the analysis he suggests for sentences. At this point I will discuss only the first issue Diamond brings up, leaving the second one for chapter 8.

If we permit incomplete definitions, Diamond claims, then we will have to give up logic. Very briefly, Diamond argues as follows. Predicates that are not defined everywhere should be understood analogously with fuzzy proper names that we introduce into language through a description that is true of more than one object. Although it is possible to play with proper names and search for a logic that will define the relations between them, it turns out that such a logic would have catastrophic implications. Extending this argument to predicates that are not defined everywhere, and are thus similar to proper names, yields the same conclusion for these predicates.

Let us say the name "Paradise Wood" denotes one forest near Monymusk in Aberdeenshire. If this were the only forest in the area, Diamond claims that there would be no problem. Nevertheless, there are some true sentences that one can assert about Paradise Wood "despite the absence of sharp boundaries." For example "Paradise Wood is a forest" is a true sentence.[12] Similarly, if all forests have more than 100 trees, then we could naturally assert, "Paradise Wood has more than 100 trees." We can now deduce a general principle. If all the forests in our area have property $P(\ )$ in common, then the sentence "Paradise Wood is P" is true. But here Diamond argues that once we make such natural expansions, there may be chaos in our deductive system. According to this logic, sentences such as "Paradise Wood has a certain number of trees" will be true, but "Paradise Wood has X trees" is false for every X.[13]

Diamond claims that an analogous problem exists in the case of a predicate that is not defined everywhere. The analogue of the previous

---

[12] Here Diamond adds an extremely important note concerning Frege's conception of reference: "But there will also be some sentences containing the name of the wood to which we cannot assign a determinate truth-value. If there were not such sentences, 'Paradise Wood' would refer in a decent Fregean way to a single object and not to a logically fuzzy one" (Diamond 1995, p. 147). I shall return to this issue in chapter 6.

[13] The chaos in logic that Diamond is warning of here is strongly reminiscent of similar problems that we face in supervaluation (see van Frassen 1966). Put in this terminology, Diamond's discussion does not allow any middle path between ordinary truth and mere formal truths that we generate by the method of supervaluation. I hope that the lacuna in this view will become clear by the end of chapter 8.

principle which makes it possible to assign a truth-value to sentences that mention such a predicate is the fuzzy principle, which states, "A proposition that mentions a partially defined predicate P is true if all the concepts that expand P and that are defined everywhere satisfy the proposition." For example, if we call someone who believes both p and q a deist and someone who believes neither a non-deist, then we have a concept with sharp boundaries that is not defined everywhere. In order to deal with sentences that contain a predicate of this sort, we must examine all the predicates E that are expansions of it and share the range on which it is defined as either true or false. If every sentence obtained by substituting such an E for P is true, then and only then is the sentence mentioning P true. But Diamond shows that, even though an axiom of this sort allows us to treat partially defined predicates as though they were completely defined from a logical standpoint, it leads to a problematic situation. For example, the law $P \vee \neg P$ will be valid even for an expression that is not defined everywhere, and even if none of the disjuncts are true (Diamond 1995, p. 169). As a result we will obtain all sorts of artificial truths that will force us to distinguish between situations in which a logical principle is valid and those in which it is not. Diamond is not saying that a fuzzy logic of partial expressions will lead to a contradiction, but that it will create a degree of complication that logic cannot tolerate. Logic, like geometry, requires a certain amount of idealization. Here Diamond makes use of Frege's simile that a logic of concepts that are not defined everywhere, like a geometry of knots and ropes rather than points and lines, is impossible.

One immediate question that arises here is: what is wrong with a geometry of knots and ropes? A logic of partially defined concepts would most likely be more complicated than a logic of completely defined concepts, but is this a reason for saying that it is not a logic? For those who truly believe in the reality of incompletely defined concepts, the claim that there must be some idealization that will make logic simpler is not sufficient to eliminate them. From this viewpoint logicians who refuse to accept incompletely defined concepts are like physicists who refuse to accept the existence of friction in order to promote a better idealization. I for one have no doubt that it is possible to propose a logic of partially defined concepts, as I present one in the following chapter, and I believe it will prove fruitful for analyzing expansions in general. Moreover, Frege's comment seems to me more applicable to vague concepts, which lead to absurdities and not only difficulties in making logic general and simple.

Indeed, the lack of seriousness with which Frege treats the idea of concepts that are not defined everywhere, as Diamond sees it, is already prominent in the very notion that such concepts need to be saved by the fuzzy principle.[14] Moreover, Dummett's idea, which was mentioned above, that predicates for partially defined concepts need to be "specified," as if they referred in some non-specific way to some completely defined concept or set of such concepts, begs the question. The analogy between a name like "Paradise Wood" and a function which is not defined everywhere seems artificial to me.[15] Few people, I believe, will agree that the fact that addition is not defined for Clinton is evidence that addition is not a real function or that "$2 + 7 = 9$" is not a perfectly good sentence.

I would now like to comment on the problem of compositionality mentioned in Diamond's second argument against the possibility of partially defined concepts. Diamond claims, quite convincingly, that a sentence like "Paradise Wood is a forest" is true, but not in the same sense that "Socrates is Greek" is true. There is no decomposition of the former sentence into components which give rise to the truth of the sentence as there is in the case of the latter sentence. The sentence gets its meaning all at once, as if it were a simple symbol. This is a very important point, since it implies that the existence of expansions contradicts Frege's paradigm of logical analysis, according to which we have to decompose sentences into their elements and give each element a reference or some other value, so that the truth or falsity of the sentence, as well as its meaning, will be dependent on this decomposition. Thus Diamond's previous argument about the complexity of a logic with predicates that are not defined everywhere suggests another, more substantial argument: partially defined concepts are problematic not merely because they require a complicated logic, but because they force us to abandon the very notion of the decomposition of sentences.

The problem with this description is that it is hard to see why we should accept the view that sentences which contain partially defined predicates

---

[14] I am indebted to Hili Razinsky for this comment.

[15] Let me just note briefly that the term "Paradise Wood" belongs to the same category of imaginary words that are required in order to apply the existential instantiation (EI) law in first-order logic (see chapter 6). The analogue of this term in the case of concepts is an imaginary predicate that is required in order to apply the corresponding law in second-order logic. This is exactly what is suggested by Dummett (1973, pp. 170–1), where he equates partially defined concepts with definite descriptions on a higher level (e.g., "what Frederick has always wanted to be") that fail to refer (because there are several things that Frederick has always wanted to be).

must obtain their truth-value as if they were simple unstructured expressions. As noted above, if the legitimacy of partially defined concepts is accepted, it becomes clear that sentences whose elements refer to such concepts obtain their truth-value directly.[16] Secondly, even if we admit that the sentence "Paradise Wood is a forest" is a non-decomposable string, thus differing from a sentence such as "Socrates is Greek," we should not conclude from here that the last sentence cannot be analyzed at all. Just for comparison: when we read the mathematical sentence "$dy/dt = 6$" in the usual way and we do not yet decompose it to "dy" and "dt," this does not imply that it is not analyzable. I return to this issue in chapter 8.

Diamond's last argument actually involves the problem of *expanding* partially defined concepts, not merely the problem posed by such concepts in and of themselves. This implies that a sentence obtained by the expansion of a concept – by the fuzzy principle or any other one – will contain expressions that are found in ordinary sentences, but the contribution of the expressions to the truth-value of the two types of sentences will be different. In the case of an expanded concept we cannot speak about what a particular expression signifies independently of the sentence in which it appears, and we cannot assume that proper names or predicates appearing in different sentences will have the same meaning. The third argument develops this intuition in a different direction.

EXTENSIONALISM AND EXPANSIONS

In contrast to the first two arguments, the third one seems to me to be valid; its assumptions are the basic requirements of any extensionalist logic. A predicate must denote the same concept throughout the concept's development, even if the concept denoted by the predicate undergoes changes. Assume that we give expressions references, or other semantic values that satisfy laws similar to those satisfied by references, and examine the coherence of the expression "the development of a concept." Expanding the concept under discussion means changing the truth-value – the reference – of the sentence: a concept denoted by $P(\ )$

---

[16] If the world were different then a partially defined concept might be completely defined. In that case it would be possible to use the ordinary methods to decompose sentences containing expressions that denote partially defined concepts. Diamond's position implies that the syntactic properties of a sentence are dependent on the external situation.

which was undefined for the object denoted by "*a*" will now be true. But if the reference of the sentence is a function of the references of its components, and the predicate and the name "*a*" denote the same reference, we are left with a contradiction: the truth-value of the sentence, which was not "true" when the concept was not defined everywhere, will be "true" after the concept is expanded.

This argument appears almost explicitly in Frege's writings. The sentence "−4 has a square root" changes from false to true when the system of real numbers is expanded to the system of complex numbers. If the signs denoted the same concepts, a false sentence would become a true sentence, which contradicts the claim that the truth-value of a sentence is a function of the reference of the expressions composing the sentence. This is the reason that Frege writes: "If we allow such talk then sentences which meant the True before the shift, mean the False afterwards. Former proofs lose their cogency. Everything begins to totter" ("Logic in Mathematics," in Frege 1979, p. 242). This argument does not involve any of Frege's assumptions about thoughts or the nature of concepts. Even his realism does not play an important role here. Frege's logical analysis is based on the ascription of references to predicates, sentences, and names, which are ruled by the immutable principle that substitution of equals for equals in a complex expression does not change the reference of the expression. It seems that any view that adopts this basic idea must stand in opposition to the notion of the development of concepts. Thus, anyone who believes, like Quine, that the work of concepts can be performed just as well if they are *simply* replaced by their extensions, cannot capture the idea of the development of concepts. This is because, unlike mere replacement of one concept by another, the very idea of development requires that the concept remains the same throughout its changes. This conflicts with the identity criteria of extensions, which are, in fact, sets or classes.

This argument underlies Frege's metaphorical remark that logic cannot deal with "quasi-conceptual constructions that are still fluid." If we accept the idea that linguistic expressions refer to something, and add the requirement that the substitution of an expression for another one with the same extension does not change the reference of the complex expression in which it is substituted, then it seems impossible to question Frege's view. It seems that not only Frege's realism but also his principles of logic prevented him from accepting the development of concepts. This argument led Frege to the conclusion that "the progress of the history of the sciences runs counter to the demand of logic. We must distinguish between history and system. In history we have development; a system is static" (Frege 1979, p. 242).

CHAPTER 3

The grammar of constraints

As we have seen, Frege absolutely excluded expansions from the realm of logic, because he claimed that logic involves the laws of truth, and truths are not developed, but can only be derived from other truths. But then we remain with the question about what to do with the process that other mathematicians and philosophers describe as "expanding a concept." Two alternatives were suggested by Frege. The first, which considers expansions to be changes within the thinking subject, was criticized above. The second alternative is that the original concept has simply been replaced by a new one.

My intention in this chapter is to present an analysis of non-arbitrary expansions. I will begin with a criticism of Frege's second alternative, which can then be generalized to a description of the development of concepts in terms of embedding a given model into a richer one. This emendation leads to the main section of this chapter, which presents a framework for introducing several kinds of non-arbitrary internal expansions, and closely examines the issue of the completeness of certain logics that arise naturally out of the consideration of expansions.

BETWEEN REPLACEMENT AND GROWTH OF CONCEPTS

The third argument discussed in the previous chapter makes it clear why Frege insists that concepts do not develop, but rather that one concept is replaced by another. But even though this description provides somewhat of a solution to the problem, it raises even more difficult problems. Even if Cantor's concept of number is different from the one held by Gauss, we still need to know *how* the two concepts are different. They are unlikely to be as different as the concepts "tiger" and "table." Frege himself tries to address this problem:

Of course this is an inexact way of speaking, for when we come down to it we do not alter a concept; what we do rather is to associate a different concept word or concept sign – a concept to which the original concept is subordinated (Frege 1979, p. 242).

Here Frege is clearly trying to describe the relation between the old and the new concept as one of subordination. This is, however, an incomplete description of what is involved in non-arbitrary expansions of concepts. The concept "cucumber" is subordinate to the concept "vegetable," but the concept "vegetable" is not a natural expansion of the concept "cucumber."

When we speak about the expansion of a concept we are talking about two concepts such that one of them *grew out* of the other. The attempt to describe this as subordination is far from capturing the organic-like connection between the concepts. Indeed, in order to capture this connection we must realize that a concept which was defined on some objects is now defined on a broader range of objects, and – what is more important – that the expansion itself is not arbitrary. In Frege's system, however, this statement, which only begins to describe what happens in many expansions, cannot even be formulated.

Frege's suggestion is problematic in another area as well. If the only thing involved in the transition to complex numbers, infinite numbers, and differentials were a substitution of one concept for another, then how can we explain the mathematical community's opposition to these "substitutions," which was sometimes quite intense? Frege himself, in earlier writings, claimed that complex numbers lead to non-intuitive conclusions. If the concepts are simply different, then the quest for intuitiveness in expansions is illusory (just as one should not try to withdraw money at a river's edge because it is called a bank).

Modern logic suggests a much better technical alternative than Frege's notion of subordination. Tarski's notion of *truth in a model* suggests that we view expansions as the embedding of one model within another. This suggestion is more promising than Frege's, if only because it points in the directions of systems of concepts and the laws that apply to them, rather than being local, as is the Fregean system with its restriction to sentences and predicates. Indeed, even when we perform an expansion on one undefined point, say in the case of "$2^0 = 1$", we never use only the one sentence at hand, but consider other areas of our knowledge to help us decide the truth-value of the sentence under discussion. Secondly, within Tarskian models we can discuss external expansions where we add objects to our world. Such a possibility does not exist in Frege's logic.

The notion of embedding, however, does not suffice to capture the complexity that we find in non-arbitrary expansions. Even if certain expansions, such as that from the natural numbers to the integers or from the real numbers to the complex numbers, are examples of embedding, not all types of embedding are expansions.[1] Any model can be embedded within a broader one. What needs to be added to the idea of embedding to adapt it to the idea of expansion is the stipulation that the new model is *obtained* from the old one.

Here we can call on such notions as model completeness or Cohen's forcing, which we mentioned towards the end of chapter 1. These notions, however, do not capture (nor were they designed to capture) expansions of concepts, but only expansions of domains (external expansions). We therefore need to design a framework in which expansions of functions can be studied.

THE FRAMEWORK

To begin with, we need to generalize the Tarskian definition of truth to allow for models of a *first-order language* L which include functions with undefined points. One way to do this is to add a new object to every model X and to define "$f(a) = X$" as true wherever $f(\ )$ is not defined for a. The definition of truth for models that allow partially defined functions parallels Tarski's classical definition. Thus, a language $L(X)$ is a set that includes:

1. Function-symbols: $\{f_i j : i \in T, j \in S, T$ and S are a subset of the set of natural numbers $\mathbb{N}\}$; with the intention that $f_i j$ is a j-place function. In real cases, where the function and the number of its places are clear – such as "$+$", "$-$", "$\times$" – I shall omit the indices and use the generally accepted symbols.
2. A set of object symbols: $\{K_i : i \in T, T$ a subset of $\mathbb{N}\}$.
3. An infinite set of variables V.
4. An identity symbol --"$=$"-- and connectives "$\rightarrow$", "$\wedge$", "$\vee$", "$\neg$", "$\forall$", "$\exists$", "(", ")."
5. A symbol "$\underline{X}$", which will designate X.

The set of terms in $L(X)$ is defined by induction: every object symbol is a term and every variable is a term. Every iteration of a function symbol on an ordered set of terms with the appropriate number of terms is also

---

[1] In the case of infinite models, it is also possible for a model to be nested within itself.

a term. The symbols f, h, and g will be used as schematic letters over function symbols, a, b, and c for names of objects different from X, and x, y, and z as schematic letters for variables.

Given a set of objects M, we can define an interpretation of L in M as a function H from L to M which assigns to every object symbol an object from M and to every function symbol a partial function from an appropriate product of M into M.

Truth in a partial model is defined in the following natural way: first, it is posited that "$h(X) = X$" is true for every function h.

Given an interpretation of L in M and an assignment σ which takes the set of variables V into M and two terms in L, say two-place terms $f(x, y)$ and $g(x, y)$, we define:

$$\text{```}f(x, y) = g(x, y)\text{' is true in } M\text{''}$$

iff either the terms f and g are defined for $(\sigma(x), \sigma(y))$ and are equal or if they are both undefined for $(\sigma(x), \sigma(y))$.

Each atomic formula has a truth value and connectives which can be defined naturally. The quantifiers are allowed to range over every element in the model and X is not allowed to be a possible value; hence, $f(a) = \underline{X}$ does not entail $\exists y(f(a) = y)$, and this enables us to express the fact that the function is not defined on a certain point a by writing "$\neg\exists y(f(a) = y)$." A proof of the completeness of this logic, which we will call "$L(X)$," can be found in Mikenberg (1977).

Note that when the function 2^y is not defined on 0 but is interpreted as the power function, say in the set of positive natural numbers, then $2^{z-y} = 2^z{:}2^y$ is not true, for in some cases (when $z = y = 1$) one side is not defined while the other is. Rather, what can be held is the following:

1. $\forall z \forall y [(2^{z-y} \neq \underline{X} \ \& \ 2^z \neq \underline{X} \ \& \ 2^y \neq \underline{X} \ \& \ 2^z{:}2^y \neq \underline{X}) \rightarrow 2^{z-y} = 2^z{:}2^y]$.

In other words, known general equations can be held under the condition that all the terms are defined. It is now possible to present the following definitions.

Definition 1: Internal expansion

Let M and N be interpretations of a language $L(X)$. N is defined as an "internal expansion of M" if M has the same set of elements as N and the functions in N coincide with the functions in M and possibly define them on additional values. In this case we shall write "$N \gg M$.[2]"

Definition 2: Forced internal expansion

Let S be a set of sentences. An internal expansion $N \gg M$ is forced by S if:

1. S is true in M.
2. S is true in N.
3. Every model K that is an internal expansion of M, and for which S is true, is compatible with N, i.e., the functions in N and K agree on their common part.

Examples

It is easy to check that the examples of expanding the power function to the zero and the negative numbers, and even to the rational and the real numbers, are captured by the definitions above. We only have to supply the appropriate laws S and models M, N. For example:

$M =$ The partial model of the field of real numbers where the power function 2^x is defined for natural numbers. The language $L(X)$ includes $\{1, 0, +, -, x, :, 2^x\}$.
$N =$ The internal expansion where the power function is defined on all integers.
$S =$ The sentence (1) as defined above.

Another example is the expansion of the trigonometric functions from $\frac{1}{2}\pi \geq \theta \geq 0$ to the real numbers. S is taken here as the set of sentences:

1. $\cos(x + y) = \cos(x)\cos(y) - \sin(x)\sin(y)$.
2. $\sin(x + y) = \sin(x)\cos(y) + \sin(y)\cos(x)$.

The models M, N and the language are defined naturally. Here too (as with 1) we must include the condition that the expressions are defined.

A further example is the expansion of the relations "X has the same number as Y" and "X has more elements than Y" to infinite sets (I am using this formulation rather than the definite description "The number of elements in X" in order to circumvent problems of abstraction).

---

[2] $M \gg M$ is always true, however.

The expansions of these relations can also be viewed as internal forced expansions.

M = The collection V of all sets, and the language is the epsilon relation and a two-place function defined for *finite* sets $f(S, T)$ as follows:
If S has the same number of elements as T then $f(S, T) = 1$.
Otherwise define $f(S, T) = 0$.
If either S or T is infinite, then $f(S, T)$ is undefined.
N is the internal expansion of $f(\quad, \quad)$ to all sets in V.
R is the following law:

$f(S, T) = 1$ iff there is a one-to-one correspondence between S and T.

It is easy to check that N is forced by R.

We now arrive at an interesting phenomenon in the theory of expansions. Every forced expansion is determined once there is a fixed set of constraints, yet sometimes an alternative expansion can be suggested. This may be the case when a *different* set of laws is taken as the constraints. An example may prove useful here.

Definition 3

Assume that F and G are two functions defined from a set K to a set B. The function F is said to be greater than or equal to the function G if the image of F includes that of G.

Definition 4

The cardinal number of the set K is smaller than the cardinal number of the set B if (i) there is a function F from K to B; (ii) there is an element u in the set B not included in the image of F; and (iii) there is no function G greater than F that contains u in its image. See figure 1.

On the basis of this definition, which is an intuitive characterization of "K has a smaller number of elements than B," I suggest an alternative definition for "K has the same number of elements as B."

Definition 5

A set K has the same cardinal number as the set B if the cardinal number of K is not smaller than that of B and the cardinal number of B is not smaller than that of K.

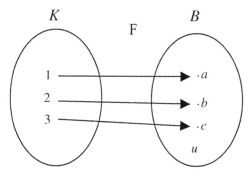

Figure 1.

Proposition 1

Cantor's expansion of "the set A has the same number of elements as B" and the expansion of the same expression in definition 5 above are incompatible.

Proof
I shall prove that, according to definition 5, the set of all subsets of N – namely, $P(N)$ – has the same cardinal number as N. To verify this, we only needed to see that it is not true that the set of natural numbers is greater than $P(N)$ and that it is not true that it is smaller. The latter, which is the interesting case, is easy to demonstrate. For every function F from N to $P(N)$ and for every counterexample element u (for example, the one constructed by the diagonal argument), a greater function G that includes it can be defined. QED

This invites a whole set of mathematical questions as to whether a forced expansion is the only forced one (to be discussed below). But first let us consider the following definition.

Definition 6: Strongly forced expansion

We say an internal expansion $N \gg M$ of a language $L(X)$ is *strongly forced* by S if:

1. $N \gg M$ is forced by S.
2. Every way of forcing an internal expansion using a set of sentences from $L(X)$ is compatible with N.

One may question, however, whether there are any strongly forced expansions. The following is a theorem which guarantees that theoretically this is not an empty concept.

Proposition 2

If N is an internal expansion of M which is forced by S and the theory of M is the same as the theory of N, then S strongly forces the continuation.

Proof
Assume a different expansion $K \gg M$ forced by T which is not compatible with N. T is true in N, but according to the assumption, N is not compatible with K; this shows that T does not force an expansion, contrary to our assumption. QED

If M and N have the same theory, then it is most likely that strongly forced internal expansions will be found. But since this only occurs in some superficial cases, it is better to define a more general concept.

Definition 7: Forcing relative to Γ

Let Γ denote a set of laws true in M. We say that a forced expansion $N \gg M$ by S is strongly forced relative to Γ if S is a subset of Γ and all ways to force an expansion using laws from Γ coincide.

Thus instead of proposition 2 we have the following one, which is also easy to prove.

Proposition 3

If N is an internal expansion of M which is forced by S, and Γ is true in M and in N, then N is strongly forced by S relative to Γ.

Proof
Assume a forced expansion $K \gg M$ by a set of sentences A from Γ, which is not compatible with N. A is true in N, but A is also true in K, which is incompatible with N. This shows that A does not force an internal expansion.

Example

Let us take D to be the set of all equations that hold for the rational numbers. We assume that the equations in D are written in a language $L = (1, +, -, \times, 2^x)$ (interpreted as plus, minus, times, and the power function). Take the expansion of the power function from the rational numbers to the real numbers. This is strongly forced with respect to D.

Indeed, if T is an equation that forces an incompatible expansion K, then T is true in K. But T is true also in the real numbers. For if an equation is true of the rational numbers then it remains true after a completion of the power function to the real numbers (this is so because all the functions that are written in our language are continuous, and if $s(x) = g(x)$ is well defined and true for every rational number, then the limits of $g(x)$ and $s(x)$ also coincide). Now, since the expansion by T is forced, it must be compatible with N, which also satisfies T. It follows that the expansion of the power function is strongly forced with respect to D.

The different concepts of non-arbitrary expansion can help us understand the nature of indefiniteness, which so far I have only designated by X. The meaningless points of the model can be classified according to the type of non-arbitrary expansion, if there is any, that provides them with meaning.

Definition 8: Forced meaninglessness

Assume that $f(\;\;)$ is not defined for a.

1. $f(a)$ is a removable point if it is possible to define it by a forced internal expansion.
2. $f(a)$ is strongly removable if it is possible to define it via a strongly forced internal expansion.
3. $f(a)$ is arbitrary if it is not possible to assign it any forced meaning.
4. $f(a)$ is essentially indefinable with respect to S if its meaninglessness is forced by S – if there is no (internal) expansion that preserves S and assigns a meaning to $f(a)$.

This is the case with the symbol "$1/0$," where the very act of giving the symbol a value, together with some laws, implies a contradiction. This suggests a way to prove that a certain symbol is undefined or meaningless with respect to some laws or constraints. Nevertheless, it may happen that $f(a)$ is essentially indefinable with respect to some set of sentences T and at the same time is a removable point.

LOGICS OF EXPANSION

Let us now enrich the language of first-order logic to include expressions of the form "$F(T, h(x)=y)$," where T is a sentence in L and $h(\ )$ a function symbol in L. Given a model M and an assignment σ, the formula "$F(T, h(x)=y)$" is true in M if:

A. T is true in M.
B. There is an internal expansion of M, say G, in which $h(x)=y$ and T is true.
C. Every internal expansion of M in which $h(x)$ is defined and which satisfies T satisfies $h(x)=y$.

Having defined this interpretation we get a logic $L(F)$ which is incomplete.

Proposition 4 (Saharon Shelah)

$L(F)$ is not complete.

Proof
To show this let us write a sentence that is true only in the standard model of arithmetic. Define $L(X)=\{0, +, \times, S(\ ), \underline{X}\}$ and add a symbol $f_\mathrm{p}(\ )$. To the collection of accepted requirements on addition, multiplication, and the successor function we add the requirement that every number except zero has an immediate successor and an immediate predecessor. We also add "$f_\mathrm{p}(0)=1 \wedge \forall y\,(y \neq 0 \rightarrow f_\mathrm{p}(y)=\underline{X})$." Call the conjunction of this set of sentences R. Now write:

1. $\forall x(f_\mathrm{p}(S(x))=0 \rightarrow f_\mathrm{p}(x)=0)$
2. $\forall x(f_\mathrm{p}(x)=1 \vee f_\mathrm{p}(x)=0 \vee f_\mathrm{p}(x)=\underline{X})$

and call T the conjunction of 1 and 2. Let K be a model for R. K contains the set of natural numbers and perhaps other numbers. Now for every natural number x, but for no non-standard number, it is true to say:

$$F\,(T, f_\mathrm{p}(x)=1) \quad \text{is true in } K.$$

For every standard natural number there is a model in which it is defined as 1 and T is preserved. Every model which expands M and in which T is true must define h as 1. If it defines h as 0, yet preserves T, then due to the first sentence of T we will obtain a descending series that will reach 0, where the function will be defined as 0. But this is a contradiction. If, however, we have a non-standard number, then we can define it as 0 while preserving T. Thus the sentence "$R \wedge \forall x F(T, f_p(x) = 1)$" is true only in the standard model of arithmetic. According to the incompleteness theorem, $L(F)$ is incomplete. QED

With a weaker interpretation of "$F(T, h(x) = y)$" we can obtain a better result. Given a family of models M_i such that 0, $i \in I$, let M_0 denote the model from which all the expansions proceed, while every other model in the family is an internal expansion of M_0.

Define the operator F as follows. Given an assignment for the variables, "$F(S, h(x) = y)$" is true in the family $M(I)$ of models iff:

1. $h(x)$ is not defined in M_0.
2. S is true in M_0.
3. There is a model in the family in which both S and $h(x) = y$ are true.
4. For every model in the family in which $h(x)$ is defined and S is true, $h(x)$ is defined as y. Let us call this logic $L(\text{WF})$.

Proposition 5 (Saharon Shelah)

$L(\text{WF})$ is weakly complete.

Proof

Given a sentence A in the language $L(\text{WF})$, we can write a first-order sentence A^* such that A has a model iff A^* also has one. This will entail that the question of whether a sentence B is logically true or false is reducible to a similar question in the first-order language. Given a sentence A in the language $L(\text{WF})$, we define the language L^* as follows:

a. Add to L two one-place predicates $P(\ )$ and $Q(\ )$ (the idea is that P will capture the elements of M_0 and that the elements that satisfy $Q(\ )$ will be the representatives of the models in the family of models that expand M_0 internally).
b. For every n-place function $f(\ )$ there is an $(n+1)$-place function $f^*(\ )$ (the idea is to allot the places as follows: the first place is for the representative from Q of the internal expansion belonging to the family,

while the other places are for describing the behavior of the function $f(\ )$ in that model).

c. For every n-place relation $R(\ )$ in L, there is an $(n+1)$-place relation $R^*(\ )$.

d. Add a new constant C^* that denotes M_0 and satisfies $Q(C^*)$.

Assume that A is a true sentence in the family of models M_i, $i \in I$. Let us define a model for the language L^* as follows:

$$G = P^G \cup Q^G$$

where $\varnothing = P^G \cap Q^G$.

The function $f^*(j, a_1, a_2, \ldots, a_n)$, where j belongs to I and $a_1, a_2, \ldots, a_n$ belong to M_0, is defined as the value of the function f in the model M_j. Moreover, $f^*(C^*, a_1, a_2, \ldots a_n)$ is defined in the same way as $f(\ )$ is defined in M_0.

We can show by induction that $\varphi(a_1, a_2, \ldots)$ is true in M_i when $a_1, a_2, \ldots$ belong to M_0 iff $\varphi^*(i, a_1, a_2, \ldots)$, which is obtained by replacing every function symbol $f(\ )$ by the respective symbol $f^*(i, \ldots)$ and every relation symbol $R(\ )$ with $R^*(\ )$, is true in G. QED

We can show that the expression "$F(T, h(a) = b)$" has a different logic from other forcing relations that generalize Cohen's. Indeed, this follows from the fact that $F(T, h(a) = b \vee g(c) = d)$, when defined in a natural way, does not entail $F(T, h(a) = b) \vee F(T, g(c) = d)$.

FURTHER DEVELOPMENTS

I will end this chapter with one implementation, that follows from what was said here for mathematics, and I will comment on the possibility of different expansions of mathematical concepts.

One issue, which I believe to be extremely important, has to do with the possibility of extending the concept of number to transfinite sets, in a method different from that of Cantor.

In this chapter I showed an example of this, in order to present the idea of a forced extension which is not strongly forced. But this raises an important question:

Is it possible to create a forced extension of finite cardinality which distinguishes between different infinite magnitudes and yet is incommensurate with Cantor's concept of infinite cardinality? The answer may have implications for the foundations of mathematics.

It would seem that this question can have a trivial answer: let us define, for any set X, the function $|X|_s$. If A is some infinite set,

$$|A|_s = \begin{cases} \aleph_0 & \text{if } |A| = \aleph_0 \\ 2^{\aleph_0} & \text{if } |A| \geq 2^{\aleph_0} \end{cases}$$

where $|A|$ is the usual von Neumann definition of cardinality.

Given this "answer," however, it is clear we have to formulate our question more carefully, and this is by no means an easy task.

I do think the answer to our question can be in the affirmative, and I will permit myself to mention the following proposition here without proof.

There exists a notion of cardinality $|\quad|_1$ such that every set A and B satisfy the following conditions:

1. For a finite set A, $|A|_1 = |A|$.
2. For every ordinal α, β if $\text{ZFC} \vdash |A| = \alpha \wedge |B| = \beta, \alpha \neq \beta$, then ZFC $\vdash |A|_1 \neq |B|_1$.

If, however, $A = P(\mathcal{N})$, then $|A|_1 = |V|_1$, where $\mathcal{N}$ is the set of all natural numbers, and $V = \{x \mid x = x\}$, i.e., the class of all sets.

As mentioned, this concept of number has implications for the foundations of mathematics. Gödel suggested that, of all possible classes, cardinality should be the criterion for determining which are legitimate sets. According to this criterion, the class A is a set iff $|A| < |V|$.

If we adopt this criterion in conjunction with the concept of cardinality we have been using here, then we are in a position to reject the power set axiom. The most important proponent of this position is Paul Cohen, and here we can give Cohen support from Gödel's insight. The study of the world of sets that results from this motivation, and the possible rationale for the set theory that results, lies beyond the scope of this work.

With this approach we open an interesting direction of inquiry – finding different concepts of number. This implies not only that the concept of number can be embedded in different ways within set theory (as noted by Benacerraf 1983), but that the meaning of this concept does not depend solely on our intuition.

What we have discovered about numbers can be projected on to other mathematical entities, e.g., functions. A very notable function here is $\Gamma(x)$ (see below). Can the factorial function $x!$ be expanded in some way that will yield an interesting function other then $\Gamma(x)$?

Thus the description of forced expansions is not indifferent to mathematical practice, but can in fact inspire mathematical research.

A second comment, with which I would like to finish this chapter, has to do with some concepts of expansion that are different from those suggested here, and the relations between them. The way to discover such concepts is by reflection on real expansions in mathematics, and the various ways in which such expansions can be described.

For example, expansions in the form of a Taylor series cannot be formulated as a proposition of first-order predicate calculus, but can be described in a language that allows sentences of infinite length. It would be interesting, then, to study expansions whose description requires a higher-order language, such as Lww_1 or second-order predicate calculus.

Nevertheless, there are many more types of expansions which require only first-order logic. There are examples that are not captured by the above definition, and require the introduction of a new one. Consider the expansion of the power function to the field of complex numbers while taking as S the fact that the function is analytic. Assume that $N \gg M$ and write:

1. N is an internal expansion of M in which the domain of the function $f(\ )$ is expanded. $\mathrm{Dom}(f)$ in N includes $\mathrm{Dom}(f)$ in M.
2. S is true in N.
3. S is true in M.
4. Every internal expansion K in which S is true, and which expands the function $f(\ )$ to a domain that contains the domain of $f(\ )$ in N ($\mathrm{Dom}(f)$ in K contains $\mathrm{Dom}(f)$ in N) is compatible with N.

Definition 9

If an expansion satisfies 1–4 we shall say that "N is an internal expansion that is globally forced by S."

Let M be the model C where $f(z)$ is a partial function defined for the real numbers whose value is the power function.

Let N be the internal expansion in which $f(z)$ is expanded to the entire plane and is equal to the complex power function $G(z)$.

We take S to be the law that $f(\ )$ is an analytic function. Here we must be cautious, as the function $f(\ )$ is undefined for numbers that are not real numbers. We have to make sure that the expressions are well defined.

One way to deal with this problem is to define an analytic function as follows:

For every $z \,\forall\, \varepsilon > 0 \,\exists\, \delta \,\forall\, w$ if $|w - z| < \delta$, *if the terms* $f(z)$ *and* $f(w)$ *are well defined*, then $|(f(w) - f(z))/(w - z)| < \varepsilon$.[3]

It is easy to check that :

S is true in *M*.
S is true in *N*.

Moreover, there is no model *K* in which *S* is true, and which defines $f(z)$ for every complex number, that is incompatible with *N*. For if we assume that such an internal expansion exists, then we will have two analytic functions that are defined for the entire plane and coincide on the real numbers, which is impossible.[4] Now, it is easy to show that if an expansion is forced then it is globally forced, but the converse is not true.[5]

To conclude this section, let me just note that in some cases of expansions of concepts it is not easy to discover the law that forces the expansion. One such example is the expansion of the factorial function. We know that we are looking for a function that would preserve the law:

1. $(n + 1)! = n!(n + 1)$ (which can also be written as $\Gamma(n) = \Gamma(n - 1) \times n$, where $\Gamma(n) = (n - 1)!$),

but this law does not force an expansion and does not even globally force an expansion. In fact, any arbitrary way of defining the factorial on the segment $(0, 1)$ can be developed into an expansion that is defined for every positive real number and satisfies (1). To globally force an expansion we need to add the law that $\log(\Gamma(x))$ is a convex function. And to prove that this is true, namely that there is only one function that coincides with the factorial and log convex functions and satisfies (1), is not a trivial undertaking at all.

I have presented a description of conceptual expansions and the logic that governs them. The issue has thus been advanced beyond the point where it was left by Peacock, as we now have a description that is very sensitive to the principle of the permanence of forms. We have also discovered a class of mathematical questions with the following structure:

---

[3] Note that this is not the usual definition in textbooks. Compare with Ahlfors (1979, p. 69).

[4] I arrived at this definition from a remark by Manders, and I thank him for this. For more elaboration on the passage from real to complex numbers, see chapter 6.

[5] Take the function $f(x) = 4$ on the real numbers. It is easy to prove that analyticity alone globally forces an expansion for the whole plane, but no internal local expansion is forced by analyticity.

is the expansion of the function $f(\quad)$ strongly forced? With respect to what set of laws is the function expanded in this way? More importantly, one formula, "$F(S, h(a) = b)$," can be used to represent the transition from an undefined to a defined state, and to show that such a transition is law-governed.

Now, to understand the meaning and implications of expansions, we must add a qualitative philosophical discussion to the formal treatment just presented. However, we already have one philosophical achievement – we have shown that the claim that logic cannot treat concepts which are still in the process of formation, and that there must be a sharp separation between history and logic, needs to be reexamined. This remains true even if the above treatment of conceptual expansions does not exhaust the issue but only suggests some initial steps in the direction of a solution.

Expansions as rational procedures

In this chapter I will try to advance the ideas presented in the previous chapter. First I will investigate the connection between forced expansions and logical deductions, discuss the general applicability of forced expansions, and analyze their relation to the rule-governed completion of sequences or matrices. This will support what I asserted in the previous chapter – that not only can forced expansions be described formally, but they are a special kind of rational, logical procedure. In other words, I propose not only that we can write a formalism of non-arbitrary expansions but that such expansions are immanently linked to logic. I complete the chapter with a section on the source of the productivity of forced expansions, which will help us judge which of several possible expansions is the most promising one.

THREE CHARACTERISTICS

The claim that forced expansions are rational, logical procedures seems to require a discussion of the nature of rationality and logic. For that purpose, however, it would be necessary to take a stand on controversial issues that would take us far away from the limited topic of the present book. Instead, I have chosen to list three characteristics of forced expansions that are uncontroversially accepted as characteristics of rational procedures. If anyone prefers to keep the term "logic" for something narrower, I am willing to concede that forced expansions do not constitute a logical procedure *par excellence*, but only something resembling such a procedure.

Expansions and deduction

Prima facie there is a great difference between forced expansions and logical deductions. In the latter the conclusion is well defined before the proof, which is used only to determine its truth-value, while in an expansion we ascribe a meaning to an expression. Another indication that expansions differ from deduction is the fact that an expansion does not always preserve all the laws that were valid before the expansion, while a deduction always does. And finally, if a forced expansion were a kind of a deduction, then the possibility of forced expansions that are not strongly forced would entail that our knowledge before the expansions took place was inconsistent – which is obviously not the case.

In spite of all this, it is possible to demonstrate that non-arbitrary expansions of a certain type are equivalent to deductions. To show this we have to define a concept of expansion that is stronger than the concepts of forced expansion defined above. This new concept will take into account the possibility that the expansion may involve models with more elements than the original one. As a rule we can say that the richer and more varied the model in which we want to expand a function, the harder it is to achieve a forced expansion. In other words, if the sentence "$F(S, h(a) = b)$" is true in the model M, and N is an expansion of M, then we cannot conclude that "$F(S, h(a) = b)$" is also true in N.[1] Let us assume that we want to expand a function $h(\ )$ defined on a subset of a particular model M. When we have found the laws S that this function satisfies, we look for a forced expansion of the function, and we find the natural candidate H. H is an internal expansion of M, and in order to see if the appropriate expansion of $h(\ )$ is forced, we have to check all the expansions K that preserve S. If the model N contains M, then we must check H against many more alternatives for expanding $h(a)$ and preserving S. Therefore we cannot be sure that an expansion which was forced in the case of M will remain a forced expansion in the new case as well.

It might be useful to present an example, even if it is somewhat artificial. Assume that we want to expand the square root function, which for some reason is not defined for the number 4. Assume that the only law we have is:

$$A.\ f(y) \times f(y) = y$$

where $f(\ )$ denotes the square root function and "$\times$" denotes the

---

[1] Although the converse is generally true. If we have an internal expansion of M in which the sentence S and $h(a) = b$ are both true, and "$F(S, h(a) = b)$" is true in N, then it is also true in M.

multiplication function. If we limit ourselves to the expansion of $f(4)$ in models that contain only positive numbers, then we obtain the forced expansion "$F(A, f(4) = 2)$," which is true for the positive real numbers. But if we consider all the real numbers, including the negative ones, then the expansion is not forced, as there is another way to expand $f(4)$ (as -2) that preserves A.

But what would happen if we required that the expansion be forced when the rival expansions can be all the external expansions of the given model (i.e., all the models, including those that expand the set of elements of the given model)? This case invites the following definition.

Definition

Let M be a model of a language $L(X)$, $f(\ )$ a function defined on some of the elements of the model, and S a set of true sentences in the model. We will say that the expansion $f(a) = b$ is *absolutely forced by S* if all the expansions of M, including the external ones in which S is true, satisfy $f(a) = b$.

It is important to notice that an absolutely forced expansion is stronger than a forced expansion, yet is different from a strongly forced expansion. An absolutely forced expansion is checked against many more rival *models*, but a strongly forced expansion is checked against other *laws*.

Many examples can be given of absolutely forced expansions. The expansion of the power 2^x function to 0 that we mentioned in the previous chapter is absolutely forced by the law

$$\text{I.} \quad 2^{x-y} = 2^x{:}2^y.$$

What is interesting about absolutely forced expansions is that they are actually a kind of deduction.

Theorem

If $f(a) = b$ is an expansion that is absolutely forced by S in the model M, then the sentence $f(a) = b$ can be deduced logically from the following set of sentences:

1. The set of true atomic sentences in M and the set of sentences that are negations of the true atomic sentences in M.
2. The sentence $\exists x(f(a) = x)$.
3. S.

Proof
Assume that the sentence $f(a) = b$ is not logically deducible from (1)–(3). Then, applying the completeness theorem to the logic $L(X)$, there is a model K in which (1)–(3) are true and $f(a) \neq b$. Given such a model we can easily use it to build an expansion of M ((1) is true in K), and this contradicts our assumption that $f(a) = b$ is an absolutely forced expansion.

Moreover, applying the compactness theorem to the logic $L(X)$, we also see that $f(a) = b$ can be deduced logically from a finite subset of sentences from the union of 1 and 2 and S. QED[2]

We can thus amend the connection between deductions and forced expansions. Despite the differences between them, the two are related. Although forced expansions are weaker than deductions, they are operations of the same kind. This shows us that not only is it possible to develop a logic of forced expansions, as I showed in the previous chapter, but there is also an internal relation between the concept of expansion and the concept of deduction.[3]

Generality

In any discussion of forced expansions, we should keep in mind that this is a very widespread phenomenon – most mathematical operations have been expanded at some time, in one way or another. Moreover, these expansions take place at all levels and in all categories. Non-arbitrary expansions have been applied not only to functions of numbers, such as subtraction, division, powers, or sines, but also to functions of sets or other functions. Cantor's concept of number and Lebesgue's concept of the integral were also obtained by non-arbitrary expansions. The application of the concepts of continuity of functions and derivatives to analytic functions is another important example of a second-order expansion that was crucial for modern mathematics.

As mentioned, there are also expansions outside of logic and mathematics. Without the expansion of concepts such as instantaneous velocity,

---

[2] An interesting mathematical question is whether it can be proven that for every model M there is a model N that expands it externally in such a way that every forced internal expansion of N is an absolutely forced expansion.

[3] There are two different ways to generalize the theorem above. One way is to ask whether we can prove a parallel theorem for sentences of more complicated form than "$f(a) = b$." The second way is more philosophical, as it asks to what extent we can view certain *deductions* in natural language as forcing an expansion. The discussion in chapter 8 below pertains to this question.

modern physics could not be imagined.[4] Even in logic there are expansions of concepts. This can be seen from Hilbert's program, which proposed preserving mathematics and its treatment of infinity by seeing its theorems as ideal entities. Indeed, this was the analogy Hilbert (1983, p. 195) himself used to explain his proposal. In this view the general application of the principles of logic grew out of an older logic which was valid only for sentences of a particular type. Here the sentences of mathematics are analogous to the complex numbers, and preserving the law of the excluded middle is analogous to preserving commutativity for complex numbers.

Several attempts have been made to connect expansions with paradoxes. One was Kripke's (1975) influential suggestion that the truth predicate should be seen as not defined everywhere and as being expanded naturally to a greater range. There was also the idea that Gödel accepted when he stated that paradoxes are singular points to which the truth predicate cannot be expanded (see chapter 9). All these suggestions illustrate the connection between expansions and major topics in the philosophy of logic, as well as logic proper.

Expansions of laws

There is another extensive area of rationality which can be described in terms of the expansion of functions. When we are taking an intelligence test and are asked to extract a rule from a matrix of data and project it onto a row with one empty square, we must perform a procedure analogous to the expansion of a function within a model.[5] The extraction of an axiom from the given rows is analogous to the search for a law, while the empty square is supposed to be filled in accordingly. Such cases do not involve deduction from explicit assumptions. The matrix is not given in the form of propositions and its laws are not written down explicitly. Induction is not involved here either, since we are not searching for the answer to some already defined question, such as whether the sun will rise tomorrow. Instead, we are trying to *create* a harmonious matrix of data.

The best way to analyze the sort of rationality involved in solving matrices of this type is in terms of forced expansions. One sign that this description is appropriate is that there are sometimes matrices which can be

---

[4] See Steiner (1998) for further examples of this sort.
[5] For a study of this process from the perspective of cognitive science I refer the reader to Hofstadter (1995).

completed in more than one way, which is precisely analogous to forced expansions that are not strongly forced. In such cases the testmakers try to limit the number of alternatives by presenting a few possible answers to choose from. The fact that this sort of activity comes so naturally to us – which is clear from the very decision to use this sort of procedure to test people's intelligence – and the fact that this procedure can be analyzed in terms of expansions provide evidence for the rational nature of expansions.[6]

If we consider the relation between forced expansion and deduction, and add the facts that mathematics and physics cannot exist without forced expansions, that expansions apply to all ontological categories, and that certain analogies that we accept as diagnostic of intelligence are also a form of expansion, we obtain a strong recommendation for the position asserted here: forced expansions are a basic procedure in which human rationality is manifested. Thus, alongside deductions, analogies in general, extrapolation, and perhaps the acceptance of whatever has a high probability of being true, there is a reasoned act which is the expansion of concepts in a forced way.

HOW TO REPLY TO AN EXPANSION REJECTER

In the following chapters I will elaborate on this conclusion with questions about the nature of concepts and thoughts and the issue of realism in mathematics, but here I restrict myself to the issue of the type of rational compulsion inherent in forced expansions. One way to consider this issue is to imagine someone who refuses to accept forced expansion – call her a "forced expansion rejecter." When you show such a person a forced expansion she responds, "I can see that if you want to preserve these rules you have to accept this conclusion, but I don't want to preserve the rules or accept the conclusion, and I don't see the point of this strange game." A good way of understanding what is involved in expansions and the possibilities of this concept would be to argue with such a person.

Now, there are various ways of being an expansion rejecter. One way is to choose expansions that preserve different laws from those accepted

---

[6] The connection between expansions and the continuation of a sequence or completion of a matrix can be looked at from another angle as well. One way of reaching a definition of 2 to the zero power is to list powers of 2 in declining order one after the other and to attempt to continue the series according to the obvious rule:

$$2^5, 2^4, 2^3, 2^2, 2^1, 2^0 \qquad 32, 16, 8, 4, 2, ?$$

From this angle finding the rule to force the expansion is equivalent to continuing a sequence.

by the mathematical community. Another is to lack the mechanism that enables most people to see how to perform a forced expansion. The expansion rejecters that I am talking about are more difficult to deal with, because they are more similar to us. People who do not consider forced expansion to be a rational move agree with the rest of us that a particular expansion is forced, but see no reason to accept it. They can very well see that $\log(-1) = \pi i$ is forced by our previous state of knowledge, and are able to follow Euler's method of expanding the function, yet argue that they simply do not like the idea.

Forced expansion rejecters differ from deduction rejecters. It would be very hard for us to understand anyone who said, like Carroll's tortoise, that he accepts the assumptions of an argument and sees that the conclusion follows from them, but nonetheless refuses to accept the conclusion. Expansion rejecters can reject expansions without being accused of inconsistency. In fact, the Greeks and some sixteenth-century mathematicians were expansion rejecters, so that present-day expansion rejecters would seem at first glance to be in good company.

One answer we can give the expansion rejecter is that many excellent mathematicians objected to forced expansions but in the end were compelled to accept them, but she can still maintain her position and escape this argument in a number of ways. First, she can say that the fact that *they* accepted some expansions does not compel *her* to accept them. Second, she can claim that as soon as she sees an interesting, fruitful forced expansion she will accept the concept it produced, but this only means that she accepts the concept itself and not the forced expansion that may have led to it. In this description, forced expansions belong only to the context of discovery of the new concept, and so the process itself is not one that we are compelled to accept.

To be sure, one could claim that many forced expansions are pointless, such as Bernoulli's expansion of the log function as $\log(-1) = 0$, and therefore one should not accept any sweeping claims about the rationality of forced expansions in general, but confine such claims to the useful ones. The obvious rejoinder to this claim is that not everything that can be proven by deduction from a given system of axioms is worthwhile either. In fact, most of the valid arguments that can be constructed according to our concept of proof are pointless, but this does not lead us to infer that deduction is not a logical operation. And if we do not require all deductions to be useful or interesting in order to accept the importance of the act of deduction, why should we demand more of the concept of forced expansion?

However hard it may be to answer the expansion rejecter, it is even harder to explain the difficulty involved. For if we had a ready answer for such a refusal, then we would have a reduction of the process of expansion to some more basic procedure. We cannot argue that this sort of expansion rejecter, as opposed to other types described above, is irrational, the way Frege and other philosophers describe someone who does not accept a particular logical procedure. Note also that people who reject expansions cannot defend themselves with the argument that it is logically consistent not to accept forced expansions. Such a reaction is a non sequitur, for the one who accepts the normativity of forced expansion is not equating non-arbitrary expansions with deduction! Thus, as with other fundamental moves, it is hard to understand the opposition to the notion of forced expansions.

In such cases it may be possible to weaken the rejecters' opposition to forced expansions by making it clear in advance that we are not claiming that they are necessary in the way that deductions are. That is, we say, "If you hold the collection of rules S, and you also know that $F(S, h(a) = b)$ in the model that represents your beliefs, then you should add '$h(a) = b$' to a special store of sentences. These are sentences that you may not necessarily consider to be true, but that are special in the sense that they express your rationality and bring you closer to the truth."

Forced expansion is thus one of our accepted scientific tools. It has proved itself useful in so many cases that it is impossible to imagine modern science without it. Thus there seems no reason not to accept it as a scientific tool on a par with induction or statistical inference. The success of forced expansions encourages us to see them as a rational procedure that brings us closer to scientific truth. It is therefore worthwhile to invest our resources in the development of such expansions. We do not have to see the use of this tool as belonging merely to the context of discovery, and we do not have to wait and see what sort of concept will emerge from the expansion in order to judge its fruitfulness. Rather, the very fact that a function can be expanded in a forced way gives scientific value to the product of the expansion.

Advocating the rationality of expansions requires making a leap. If $F(s, h(a), b)$ is true in the world, then $h(a) = b$ has an important place. The hypothetical dialogue with the rejecter of the idea of forced expansions illustrates the existence of this leap, which the scientific community has repeatedly chosen to take.

But I am not claiming to know everything that can be said about this leap. It seems to me that this is just the beginning, and that there is room for philosophical discussions about forced expansions, just as there is a philosophy of deductive logic and of probability. Here I will only mention two ways of anchoring the idea that forced extensions are normative – one idealist, and the other realistic.

An idealist approach to expansions could argue that they occur on the most basic level of our experience. Every new judgment is essentially a forced expansion of a certain type. When I say that I see an oak, I am essentially expanding my existing concept of an oak to what is now present before me. This approach is based to epistemology and recalls that of Kant, which may give it other advantages as well. For example, it can be used to explain what justifies the general validity of the laws that govern our experience. Following Kant, we may suggest that we do not acquire these laws from our experience but that we force them – in the sense of the word being used here – on our experience. More specifically, to view a law of the form $\forall x(Px \rightarrow Qx)$ as constitutive of judgments of the form $h(x) = y$ is to use it in place of A in formulas of the form $F(A, h(x) = y)$.[7] If this analysis is correct, then we are actually surrounded by forced expansions, but we are only consciously aware of them when they occur in formal disciplines such as mathematics and modern physics.[8]

The realist approach to supporting the idea of expansion, which is even more appealing to me, is to show that forced expansions have proved to be a very successful tool in the real world. We may therefore hypothesize that it is a property of *our world* that it can be understood in terms of expansions. Forced expansions are rational because Nature itself seems to act in accordance with them, in the same sense as it acts in accordance with the concepts of the derivative, symmetry, and probability.

This conception allows us to preserve the difference between the normativity of expansions and that of deductions. We can put this idea as

---

[7] Quine's notion of posits follows this tradition (see his "multiplying entities" in his chapters "Posits and Reality" [1955] and "On Multiplying Entities" [1966–74], in 1977). This approach has a particular power, and I hope to examine it at another time. As can already be seen, it can be used to deal with the revisability of principles that we once thought to be a priori, or constitutive of our experience. These cases are similar to those where we have had to give up a principle that was valid in a narrow realm in order to expand the concept to a broader realm. Expanding our discourse on the world of overt phenomena to the subatomic realm or to cosmological expanses does not necessarily allow us to preserve our intuitive rules.

[8] Another, similar way of looking at this is that forced expansions occur all the time as we master our everyday language. We do not grasp all of a language simultaneously, but rather bit by bit. First we learn a few sentences, and then we learn other sentences by procedures similar to forced expansions. Hints of this idea can be found in Quine, and my student and colleague Gall Alster is studying this process in language acquisition. This approach can be supported by the argument that it is not always easy to distinguish between forced expansions and "what we have always known."

follows. When someone proves a proposition on the basis of assumptions that we accept, then either we are convinced of the truth of the conclusion, or we have to figure out why we are not. The power of a valid argument from axioms can also be explained in terms of truth: in every possible world in which the assumptions are true, the conclusion is true as well. These two aspects of the process of deduction allow us to distinguish between this process and that of forced expansions. When someone shows us that the assumptions we hold allow us to force a truth-value on a particular sentence by a forced expansion, we tend to give this sentence a privileged place in our system of beliefs. We may not accept it as true, but we distinguish it from other, ordinary sentences. But as far as their truth-value is concerned, we cannot argue that what is obtained by a forced expansion is true by virtue of this very fact alone. We can imagine possible worlds in which the sentences obtained by forced expansions are not applicable.

APPENDIX: WHAT MAKES AN EXPANSION FRUITFUL?

Forced expansions are useful in mathematics because they allow us to talk about a new area as if it were an old one. They are thus similar to analogies, in which we project a particular area, with all its relations and distinctions, onto a new one. Moreover, not only do we treat the two areas as if they were one, but the original area remains in force as part of the new one to which the new theory applies. This nesting process enables us to return to the old area with conclusions discovered in the new one, thus giving us the sense that the new area actually helps us understand the old one better.

As mentioned above, however, sometimes there is more than one way to expand the original area. This possibility raises the question of what makes one expansion fruitful and another one pointless. This question is unrelated to any metaphysical position, thus differing from the question discussed above of whether there is any point in expanding concepts in general, or the question of whether expansions are discoveries or inventions.

The question of what is responsible for making an expansion fruitful is reminiscent of the question of what aspects of a particular proof are essential to it. Once we have the proof of a theorem, we can ask which assumptions are really necessary and which can be done without. Reflection on the integers and the structure of the multiplication function led to the important concepts of ideals and rings, and to the generalization of propositions that had been proven for integers. Without this generalization we would have continued to believe that these propositions were unique to the ring of the integers. Similarly, once we have extracted the factors due to which a particular expansion has proved to be fruitful, we may be able to use this analysis to implement other expansions containing these factors. This sort of question leads to valuable mathematical insights and may demand great originality.

There are at least two different ways of answering this question. One way is to claim that there are no a priori laws for what makes an expansion fruitful. Only after an expansion has been found can mathematicians study it to see if it is fruitful. If it turns out to be so, then they continue to develop it and project it further. The other answer is that there are a priori criteria that can be applied to tell if an expansion will be fruitful even before it is investigated.

I do not know if there is actually anyone who holds either of these views as absolutely as I have described them.[9] I would like to suggest a view which is a combination of these two extremes. I do not believe either that the whole issue has to be left for an a posteriori investigation of a proposed expansion or that there can be some unambiguous criterion for deciding whether such an expansion will be fruitful or not. If we can find out what aspects of particular expansions have made them successful a posteriori, then we may be able to generalize from their success. This should advance our inquiry by sharpening our understanding of the logical source of the fruitfulness of expansions. This approach, which combines the two opposing views, seems promising. After all, mathematicians clearly do not check every possible expansion that can be suggested. They only do so when they sense in advance that a particular expansion seems fruitful and likely to lead to interersting results. Nevertheless, it is implausible to believe that, whenever mathematicians invest time and effort in investigating some particular expansion, they have some ironclad rule that guarantees in advance that the the expansion will be interesting and important.

This research is thus empirical, in the sense that it resembles chess strategies that are developed by examining many chess games and extracting the general characteristics of winning strategies. What leads to success in chess is not repeating the specific moves of previous winners but following certain general guidelines, such as focusing on the center of the board or developing one's pieces. On the assumption that the same is

---

[9] Manders (1989) seems to be close to the a priori view, and was criticized for it by Kitcher (1989).

true of mathematical expansions, I will examine successful ones, in which interesting applications of the expansions were made, and ask how the expansion facilitated the applications. I will present some examples of how this can be done.

Examples

Making distinctions

The first example I would like to analyze is the proof of the existence of transcendental numbers, using Cantor's concept of number. The only way of proving their existence that we had before Cantor was Liouville's proof, which is much more complicated than Cantor's and which requires an examination of the relation between numbers and the power of the polynomials for which they are solutions. Cantor's proof, in contrast, is amazingly simple. All it requires is the knowledge that every polynomial has a finite number of solutions and that the number of polynomials with integer coefficients is denumerable. This is enough to provide a proof that there is an infinite number of transcendental numbers, and that there are actually more transcendental than algebraic numbers.

To understand what made Cantor's expansion of the concept of number so fruitful, we should reflect upon the expansion and the proof to see what aspects of the expansion led to the construction of this new, elegant proof. Before this expansion the cardinality of some sets was called "infinite" or undefined; it was the expansion that permitted the classification of infinite sets into different types. Certain calculations showed that there is one cardinal number for the set of algebraic numbers, and a different one for the set of real numbers. And since we know that all algebraic numbers are real numbers, this constitutes a proof that not all real numbers are algebraic. Without Cantor's expansion we could not have made this classification and so we could not have achieved this elegant proof. From this analysis we may infer that the source of the fruitfulness of Cantor's expansion is the differentiation it permitted.

A similar example is the proof that $\mathbb{R}$, the set of real numbers, is non-denumerable, which is a premise of the previous proof. This can be proven by the use of Lebesgue's expansion, which preserves the σ additivity law of measure. Observing that the measure of $\mathbb{R}$ is not zero, while the measure of every individual point is zero, easily yields the proof. Here Lebesgue's expansion acted analogously to Cantor's expansion. It permitted the formulation of the law that every denumerable set has measure zero, which was necessary for this proof. At the same time, a definition of measure which would not have given every denumerable set a measure, or an expansion which would have given all sets the same measure, would not have allowed us to construct this proof.

In both of these cases, the expansion led to making distinctions, as if it had taken an unpainted surface and painted it with a variety of colors, giving us a way of demonstrating the differences between objects in the newly painted area. Note also that mere arbitrary coloring will not do. In the above examples the colors were invariant under certain natural transformations. A practical rule can now be formulated: an expansion of the concept of number that made fewer distinctions than Cantor's, or that left more sets without a number, would not be as useful. This rule would enable us, for example, to reject the expansion of the concept of number presented in the previous chapter, even though we cannot see any distinction between that expansion and Cantor's on the basis of intuition alone.[10]

Representational power

Most people unhesitatingly agree that the introduction of the zero symbol was one of the most important events in the history of mathematics. But why this is so is clearly an issue involving the methodology of expansions. The question is what we gained by introducing zero to the set of the natural numbers.

The use of the zero made it possible to handle simple algorithms in multiplication. At present, to be sure, we could formulate some other algorithm for multiplying numbers represented without the use of the zero. For example, we could use the distributive law, which does not re-quire the zero, to multiply two two-digit numbers, but it would be very cumbersome. The invention of the zero made it possible to base the multiplication of any two numbers on that of the 100 pairs that consti-tute the multiplication table (or even some subset of them, if we apply the commutative law, recall that multiplication by zero yields zero, and the like). Try multiplying two numbers written in the Roman or Hebrew system and see how complex it is.[11]

---

[10] Another use of the heuristic principle that an expansion should create the maximal number of distinctions can be found in the debate between Bernoulli and Leibniz mentioned in the first chapter. Leibniz expected his principle of making the maximum of distinctions with the minimum of rules to be valid in the case of extensions as well. From this standpoint Euler's extension is better than Bernoulli's. Another example is the factorial function. With the rule that $n \geq m \geq k$ entails that $n! \geq m! \geq k!$ and $0! = 1! = 1$ we could force $x! = 1$ for x between 0 and 1. Our rule excludes such expansions.

[11] In the Hebrew system each one of twenty-two letters of the alphabet represents a different number, so we would have to remember more that 200 multiplications by heart, even if we made use of the commutative law.

Here we should ask what is responsible for this fruitful feature of the zero. How does adding a new symbol to our system result in reducing our dependence on memorizing? The answer to this question is that the introduction of the zero allowed us to use a positional system. One important contribution of the positional system is the opportunity it created for organizing the numbers. The possibility of writing "Three hundred seventy-five" is based on a decomposition of the number into basic units (ones, tens, hundreds) which require only a small number of digits to represent them. The calculation of the decomposition of the number which is the result of the summation of the decompositions of the numbers being added is based on a simple count of the basic units of these numbers (3 hundreds, 7 tens, 5 ones). With numbers we can count trees, but with the positional system we can count tens and hundreds; that is, we can count the numbers themselves. Without the zero we could not attain such a decomposition, as we would not know what to do when a number has no (i.e., a zero number of) hundreds or tens.

The addition of the zero has therefore increased our power of representation. Another advantage of the same sort that we gain by introducing the zero is that it enables us to formulate certain laws. One basic law is that if the multiple of two numbers is zero, then at least one of the numbers is also zero; this is one of the most important algebraic laws, and an equivalent law that does not mention zero, if it were possible at all, would be very complicated to formulate.[12] The importance of this law can be seen in such a simple equation as:

$$x^2 = 2x - 1.$$

After moving $2x - 1$ to the left-hand side we obtain a factorable square and are able to solve the equation. The law which enables us to do this, and other laws which were made possible by the introduction of the zero, paved the way for the solution of non-linear equations, and thus for the invention of algebra. It is no wonder, then, that the introduction of the zero to the system of numbers occurred simultaneously with the development of algebra.

The addition of extra elements can enrich our power of representation and formulation. This can be confirmed nicely in the case of complex numbers. Considering the expansion of the real numbers to the complex numbers can help us understand the connection between expansion and

---

[12] It might look like this: If $\forall x(x + ab = x)$ then $\forall y(y + a = a)$ or $\forall z(z + b = b)$.

inductive proof. A fascinating example of this connection is Cauchy's integral formula:

$$f^n(z) = \frac{n!}{2\pi i} \int_C \frac{f(t)\,dt}{(t-z)^{n+1}}$$

where the function $f(\ )$ is analytic in an arbitrary domain D and z is a point inside a circle C which ranges over D (and $f^n(z)$ is the nth derivative).

Studying the proof shows us that even the case of $n = 0$ is difficult to prove without invoking complex numbers. If we try to formulate this theorem using ordered pairs of real numbers rather than a variable that ranges over the set of complex numbers, we will be entangled in insurmountable complications. Moreover, in such a case the connection between the nth case of the theorem and the $(n + 1)$th case would be so complicated that it might not have been discovered. The use of the complex numbers not only made the general law easy to discover but also made the transition from the nth to the $(n + 1)$th case of the theorem simple to formulate and thus provable (any reader who does not see this is invited to paraphrase the proof in Ahlfors (1979, pp. 120–3) without using complex numbers). Introducing the complex numbers has thus enriched our language and increased the number of inductive assumptions that can be formulated easily, thereby also increasing the number of propositions that can be proven by induction.

Another example that shows the power of expansions can be found in Tarski's definition of truth. It is difficult and perhaps impossible to define truth by confining ourselves to closed sentences. But by considering open sentences we can define "the formula $F(x, y)$ is satisfied by the sequence $(a, b, c, \ldots)$ of objects" and get a notion of truth for closed sentences.

Modern mathematicians have claimed that there are theories that require a specific space; Herman Weyl, for example, stated that Riemann surfaces are the "native land" in which functions "grow and thrive." Sometimes a certain space is found to be too small for a specific theory, and we therefore attempt an expansion. The question of what makes a certain space a native land for specific theorems has no easy answer, but I believe that considerations of the kind given here offer some fruitful indications.

Interpretation
The connection between expansions and their interpretations is

extremely important for a thorough understanding of their fruitfulness. There are some expansions whose interpretations preceded them and made them necessary. One example is the expansion of the rational numbers to the real numbers, which occurred after a segment of the real line was found that could not be measured. In other cases, however, the interpretation was found only after the expansion was made, as in the case of the complex numbers, which had been used for a while before Wallis showed how they could be arranged on the plane. If an expansion of the number system has a geometric interpretation, it yields a connection between algebra and geometry, making it possible to learn new things about a space from the new algebra and vice versa.

In general, every attempt at an expansion that comes in the wake of a given interpretation is a mathematical imperative that must be obeyed. The urge to expand the number system to include the irrational numbers is repeated in every example of this sort. We can live with numbers that have no interpretation, but we cannot allow any sort of interpretation – whether a magnitude, an angle, or anything else – without giving it a numerical form.

An interpretation can be fruitful in ways that were not thought of in advance. The geometric interpretation of complex numbers is important because of its connection with the concept of the angle. It is this interpretation which led to the polar representation of complex numbers and the marvelous connection between the multiplication of complex numbers and the intuitive act of rotation. Without the connection with angles the relation between the complex numbers and the plane would have remained somewhat artificial – a way of looking at them as ordered pairs with an uninterpreted multiplication operation defined on them. But once we obtained the connection between complex numbers and angles, we could produce and verify hypotheses about them, the simplest example being De Moivre's theorem and its use in providing the formulations of $\cos(n\Phi)$ and $\sin(n\Phi)$.[13]

Expansions and hypotheses
An invaluable incentive for non-arbitrary expansions is the creation of a hypothesis space. The importance of hypotheses for mathematical research is well known to all mathematicians. The art of creating

---

[13] The harmony between the field of complex numbers and the plane raises a metaphysical problem that should not be dismissed. I discuss this problem in my book *Solomon Maimon's Metaphysics: A Reconstruction* (Buzaglo forthcoming), on the harmony between spatial intuitions and numbers in Maimon's philosophy).

good hypotheses is undoubtedly one of the most important talents a mathematician can have. Now expansions enable us to create a large store of well-founded hypotheses. All the properties that had been formulated in the language of the old, narrow area are natural candidates for preservation in the broader area. Here we find that the more laws that are preserved, the more natural the hypotheses. This is because we preserve the properties needed to prove propositions in the narrower area when we moved to the broader area. For example, expanding the derivative function to the complex numbers immediately provided us with the promising hypotheses that the expressions that were valid for the derivatives of functions of real variables would remain valid for functions of complex variables.

This analysis enables us to formulate a guiding axiom for evaluating the differences in the fruitfulness of various expansions: the more laws are preserved by the expansion, the more promising it is. This rule might be helpful when evaluating two rival expansions, but it does not always agree with the rule from the first example that the more differentiation you have the better. As in Leibniz's system, the best possible mathematical structures are those that maximize the variability of our system while preserving the simplicity of our laws.

Empty expansions

Despite the fact that mathematics is rich in fascinating expansions, useless expansions are sometimes made as well. One such example is Frege's expansion of the class of names to include sentences. In the later stages of his work, Frege thought sentences were the names of truth-values in the same sense that ordinary names refer to objects. This is not an arbitrary analogy, but Dummett considers it confusing rather than useful, calling it "an unmitigated disaster."

We have to be careful here, since other expansions of properties that apply to names and objects might turn out to be valuable. Dummett is very clear on this:

We have seen that it was both natural and correct for Frege, in his extending the distinction between sense and reference from names to expressions of other kinds, to take truth values to be the referents of sentences. But we have also seen that to do so in no way obliged him to treat sentences as being a special kind of proper names (Dummett, 1973, p. 644).

Dummett's reasoning is thus that this conflation of names with sentences fails to recognize the important place of sentences in the theory of meaning. Therefore, instead of formulating the context principle by saying that the meaning of an expression is its contribution to the meaning of the sentences in which it is found, we have to say that its meaning is the contribution to the complex names where it appears, thereby losing the uniqueness of sentences. Dummett goes on to explain that Frege's resistance to partially defined concepts, which is what we are concerned with here, resulted from the pointlessness of this expansion (p. 654).

This is an interesting example of an expansion, even if it is not from mathematics. This is not only because it tells us something about Frege, but because it demonstrates that an expansion that has some technical advantages can nevertheless turn out not to be worthwhile. We are now faced with a question that is the inverse of the one we have been discussing: what makes an expansion useless?

In the example of Frege's proposed expansion, if we accept Dummett's position for a moment, the problem is that a certain field becomes homogeneous as a result of the expansion. The space of symbols denotes names, and in fact only complex names. This way we lose an important contrast: the class of sentences is assimilated into the class of names, and thus no longer has any special features.[14]

This appendix can be summarized as follows: we do not have ironclad a priori rules for evaluating expansions, but I can offer some suggestions which are worth serious consideration. One is to look for expansions that offer the greatest variability, while preserving as many as possible of the laws in the original system. Another is not to leave any interpretation without a mathematical formulation, while being careful not to assign such a formulation in an arbitrary way. A third is to try to find expansions that increase our ability to formulate new laws that could not have been formulated without them, while rejecting any expansion that erases distinctions between entities that are worth distinguishing. In addition, we should continue to investigate expansions that have already been accomplished (indeed, there are so many of them that it would take a whole book just to list them) and we should try to find other guidelines for new expansions, as this can enhance mathematical creativity.

---

[14] It would be interesting to see whether there are examples of useless expansions within mathematics. Hilbert's and van Frassen's conception of the excluded middle would probably be considered useless by intuitionists, but I cannot discuss this point here.

Implications for concepts

Once we accept the idea that forced expansions are an important manifestation of human rationality, we need a theory of concepts, reference, and thought to accommodate them. In this chapter I present a picture of this sort for the notions of concepts and reference, trying to make it as close as possible to Frege's realism and extensionalism for concepts. In chapter 8 I shall examine its implication for the notion of thought. Let me state at the outset that I do not pretend that the picture I shall propose in the following chapter is the best that could be formulated, but I do claim that it is a better idealization than Frege's. Later I will discuss the implications of forced expansions for definitions, focusing on Wittgenstein's thesis that definitions are not always feasible because of the ever-present possibility of expansion. I shall argue that the view he offers in connection with his notion of family resemblance cannot be derived from the expansion of concepts. Afterwards I will briefly examine two pictures of concepts that give an important place to non-arbitrary expansions but which are not faithful to Frege's realism.

STAGES OF CONCEPTS

If the development of concepts is not to be described merely as the replacement of one concept by another, must we accept the strange idea that the *same* concept can have different extensions? Prima facie, in the intensionalist approach to concepts, which distinguishes between a concept and its extension, there seems to be no problem with such an idea: in other possible worlds the set of tigers can be different from the one in our own world. But this does not help us understand the development of a concept in such a way that the concept remains the same despite the change in extension, because such a development does not take us from one possible world to another; rather, we remain in the same world. This gives rise to the dilemma that, on the one hand, the change in extension leads us to determine that the concept after the extension differs from what it was before, yet, on the other, we cannot accept that the difference is the same as that between two unrelated concepts. To claim that there are two different concepts is to say too little, whereas to claim that the concepts are the same is to say too much.

This dilemma can be resolved by the following proposal: a concept includes all the stages of its development. It is important to distinguish between the concept and its stages. Between one expansion and the next we have one stage of a concept, and after the expansion we have another stage of the same concept. If we take into account the possibility of expanding a concept in two different non-arbitrary ways, the stages of each concept will form a treelike structure. A division of the tree into several branches corresponds to several expansions of the concept at the same stage. What allows us to avoid Hegelian terms such as the development of concepts are the following two tentative definitions. One is that two stages A and B are on the same branch if there is a chain of forced expansions that begins at A and ends at B. The second is that two stages A and B belong to the same concept if there is a stage C such that A and C are on the same branch, and B and C are on the same branch. These definitions, which will be discussed in detail later on, make it possible to formulate what happens when a concept like the power functions is expanded. We can say that the power function as defined for the natural numbers is one stage of this function, while the expansion of this function to the rational numbers is a more advanced stage of the same function. The development of a concept is thus not an aggregate of different concepts and their extensions but a chain of links that are intimately connected to one another.

This view gives an important role to the laws that connect concepts, as they allow us to go from one stage to the next. Nevertheless, it does not imply that the extension of the concept (i.e., the set of objects on which the concept is true) is incidental to it. Since the development of a concept depends on its extension and characteristics, it is possible for the same expansion to be a forced one if the concept has one extension yet an arbitrary one if it has a different extension.[1]

The distinction between concepts and their stages helps us avoid the dilemma of whether a concept is the same or different after an expansion, but it also requires us to distinguish between concepts and sets. Concepts,

---

[1] For example, the monoticity of 2^x forces the expansion to the irrational numbers only if this function has already been defined on the rational numbers.

unlike sets, may undergo changes, and it seems that this is an important charactersitic of concepts, not a marginal feature we should ignore. It may be possible to create "concepts" that will never undergo any changes by calling the members of a random set a "concept" – by seeing a set containing a pen, a tiger, and a chocolate bar as the extension of some "$P(\ \ )$." This "concept" will never change its extension or undergo any development. But after the analysis suggested here, this may serve as an argument that this "concept" is not a true concept. Indeed, whenever a concept or function involving laws or true sentences is defined on some of the elements in the universe, we expect that it can be defined on some other elements as well. This is because the extension of a concept is generally more than just a set, and the common thread that holds the members of the set together is often strong enough to include objects outside the boundary of the set.

Immediate implications

The best way to fill in the schema outlined above is by seeing how it stands up to Frege's arguments. Surprising as it may seem, the view presented here agrees with Frege's claim that concepts do not undergo change. Although, on the current view, the extension of a concept is not a homogeneous block, but rather has a treelike structure, neither the tree nor its stages undergoes any change. From this standpoint, the idea here is a refinement of Frege's view rather than a contradiction of it, making it possible to amend Frege's first argument (as presented in chapter 2), which was found to be problematic.

It is possible to assume that concepts exist somewhere "out there" and that we ourselves try to grasp them, without finding it necessary to distinguish, as Frege does, between attempting to grasp a concept and truly doing so. Grasping a stage of a concept means being in indirect contact with the tree that includes the stage we have grasped. We thus grasp a concept by grasping one of its stages. Since the concept is a kind of chain, in order to grasp the entire chain it is sufficient to grasp one link. Thus Gauss and Cantor were holding the same chain even though each one picked it up by a different link. This formulation allows us to avoid the claim that Gauss did not grasp the concept of number, and makes it unnecessary to wait for the end of the development of mathematics, if this ever occurs, to determine that we are grasping the true concept of number, as Frege demanded.

This description leaves us with the question of what difference there is between grasping a stage of a concept and being in contact with the entire concept. How, for example, can we say that Gauss grasped the same concept of number as Cantor, when Cantor's ideas were so revolutionary? The problem is especially acute because Gauss explicitly objected to the idea of actual infinities. In general, if people grasp the concept of a factorial, do they also grasp the later expansion that $\Gamma(\frac{1}{2}) = \sqrt{\pi}$? After all, when one first learns about factorials the idea of $\Gamma(\frac{1}{2}) = \sqrt{\pi}$ is beyond one's wildest imagination, and it is possible to understand the basic concept of factorials without even knowing what π is.

This analysis is reminiscent of Kripke's and Putnam's discussion of the determination of the reference of natural kinds. When people grasped the reference of "gold" a thousand years ago they could not possibly know that its atomic number is 79, but there are good reasons for claiming that they were referring to the same thing as we are, except that they thought about it differently. What enables people with different concepts to refer to the same thing, according to Kripke, is the existence of a chain of transmission beginning with the act of pointing to a lump of gold and the word "gold" being passed on from one generation to the next. Can we claim that the situation in mathematics is similar to this one? Does the chain of extension that begins with the most elementary concept of a power preserve its reference to the same concept even though the transition from one stage to the next may include changes in our knowledge about the concept of a power?

Although this analogy, as we will see later, is helpful for the present discussion, there are some important differences between the two cases. Putnam's view, and even more so Kripke's, assumes that there is a "name" for "gold" or "iron" that we are connected to by a chain of transmissions that do not assume substantive knowledge about gold or iron. Gold and iron are available in our environment, enabling us to decide any questions we might have about them. In the case of the power functions, however, the situation seems to be more complicated, as here we refer to the function by means of a *definition* rather than by *pointing*. Therefore the idea that there is a gap between our knowledge and what we are referring to, which is easy to maintain in the case of gold or iron, is not simple in the mathematical case, even if one holds a realist view of mathematics.[2]

Moreover, if we try to insist that we all grasp the same concept, we will have to explain how this does not abolish the very notion of expansion. In other words, if we accept the realist view suggested by the analogy

---

[2] Indeed, the possibility of pointing to a set of three eggs and seeing a concrete set, as claimed by Maddy (1990), does not help us here.

with Kripke, we must assume that "$\Gamma(\frac{1}{2})$" was defined even before it was expanded just as the answer to the question about the atomic weight of gold was determined long before we knew how to ask it. This would abolish the very notion of different concept stages which we have been trying to develop. In addition, the analogy with Kripke forces us to say that those mathematicians who rejected the complex numbers because they believe that there could not be any numbers with negative squares were mistaken, since the square root of -1 actually exists. But is this a fair claim? After all, they had a proof that -1 has no square root, and it was only on the basis of this proof that we became aware of the need for the expansion to complex numbers.

There are thus some differences between Kripke's and Putnam's analysis of the reference of names and the present case, and these differences prevent the analogy from being perfect. Nevertheless, if we want to adopt a realist stance toward trees of concepts,[3] we will have to admit that someone could hold one of the stages of the concept without being able to imagine the concept's entire range. Concepts are not transparent to our minds.

I would also like to distinguish between our grasp of the stage of a concept that we are holding and our grasp of the concept itself by virtue of the fact that we are grasping one stage of it. The difference between our access to the concept stage and to the concept as a whole can be expressed as follows: we hold a stage of a concept, but we grasp the concept. This enables us to speak about different levels of grasping a concept, according to the stage we are holding. The more advanced the stage, the better our grasp of the concept, as then the concept is perceived with greater clarity. In light of this fact the difference between Gauss and Cantor can be expressed as follows: both of them grasped the same concept of number, but Cantor did so by means of his hold on a more advanced stage of the concept.

A comment on scientific revolutions

One of the most active debates in the history of mathematics – an area which has been developing rapidly in recent years – involves the question of whether Kuhn's theory of paradigm shifts can be expanded from physics to mathematics. Most historians of mathematics believe that this cannot be done. The above discussion provides us with ideas that are relevant to this debate. I have shown that the fact that two mathematicians

---

[3] Towards the end of the chapter I will abandon this assumption.

hold different stages of the same concept does not mean that the transition from one stage to the next is not a dramatic one. The transition from Gauss to Cantor was a change that cannot possibly be considered as the addition of a proof within the same axiomatic system or even the addition of an axiom to the system. Nevertheless, this does not mean that it must be considered a change of language or that mathematics before Cantor and mathematics after Cantor are incommensurable. I base this claim on the fact that the expansion of functions is a common procedure in mathematics. Even before Cantor, mathematicians such as Leibniz and Gauss knew that concepts could be expanded. Cantor's move was thus simply another step within the same methodology accepted by his opponents.

Cantor's move led to such farreaching changes that it provoked contemporary mathematicians to reexamine the basis of other theories, and raised new problems and challenges, although not to the extent that we would say that the mathematicians who preceded him and those who followed him understood the concept of mathematics differently. The expansion of the power function to the complex numbers and the expansion of numbers to infinite sets are discussed by the mathematical community within one framework. Moreover, the criteria used by Gauss and Cantor to judge the appropriateness of an expansion are common to both, even though they do not set them out explicitly.[4] Cantor's terse proof of the existence of transcendental numbers supports his view in the face of mathematicians such as Gauss, and Cantor would have felt obligated to deal with the paradoxes that Gaussians might have presented to him. This commonality is what permits us to say that Gauss grasped the same concept of number as Cantor, even if in a different way than Cantor did.

But what would happen if such a commonality did not exist? What would happen if there were one community of mathematicians that sought expansions while another community did not dare conceive of such a thing? In such a case, would we still say that the two communities grasp the same concept? The word "primitive" might be helpful here. Let us say that some tribe has a primitive attitude toward numbers in the sense that they cannot imagine that the set of numbers could be expanded. Could we then say that they have some relation to the complex numbers? Or let us say that this tribe does accept expansions, but that they use different criteria than we do. Here I am thinking of the expansion

---

[4] I became aware of this through a lecture by Itamar Pitowski on the transition between Newtonian and modern physics.

discussed (and rejected) by Aristotle in *De Anima* 403b, in which the soul is a number that moves itself, but any number of examples could be added, in the style of Goodman's "grue." In such a case we must deny that the tribe has a grasp of the whole tree of concept stages that is developed from this stage. If we say that some tribe or community does not possess the conditions that allow forced expansions in directions similar to the ones we perform, then it would be artificial to say that they are connected with the tree of stages of the concept that we grasp. This shows that the mere existence of a chain of expansions, say in the Platonic sense, is not sufficient for saying that a person who holds what seems to us to be a stage of a concept is actually referring to the entire concept of which it is a stage.

This leads to a conclusion supporting the view that there are revolutions in mathematics. The present description shows that the mathematical community has undergone a change in its attitude toward expansions. Although the Greeks vigorously opposed expansions, there has been a slow, gradual change in the mathematical community over the centuries, and at the present time we invite expansions, considering them a hidden treasure for the creation of new mathematics. Thus we can clearly say that the concept of mathematics that was held by the Greeks has undergone changes, which shows that there has been at least one revolution in mathematics.

To summarize what I have said so far, we get the following picture. I believe that the transition from Gauss's concept of number to that of Cantor did not constitute a revolution. Cantor's innovation may have been difficult for the mathematical community to accept, but this does not make it a revolution. There is, however, an important difference between Gauss and the Greek mathematicians, in spite of the fact that both of them rejected the idea of actual infinities. The difference is that Gauss permitted and even encouraged expansions, while the Greeks did not. From this viewpoint we can say that the transition from the Greek mathematicians to Gauss is importantly different from the transition from Gauss to Cantor.

Does this tell us anything about the nature of scientific revolutions? For example, how far can our discussion of the case in mathematics be transferred to the transition from Newtonian to relativistic physics? This issue requires a discussion of considerable depth, and so I will merely hint at what is involved here. The concept of momentum was defined in Newtonian physics as velocity multiplied by mass, while in relativistic physics it is defined by a more complex formula that takes into account the dependence of mass on velocity. The way we describe this change is not that momentum was once the term for a particular magnitude and now it is the term for a different one. Rather, we say that the relativistic concept of momentum is more precise than the Newtonian one. At first glance, at least, it would seems that this physical case is not really similar to the case of the expansion of the power function, because there was no change of extension in the physical case. However, there is still an appropriate sense in which we can claim that the relativistic concept of momentum was obtained non-arbitrarily from the Newtonian one. If we try to reconcile the principle of the equivalence of inertial systems with Maxwell's result that the speed of light is a law of nature, which was validated by the Michelson–Morley experiment, we necessarily end up with the Lorenz transformations and the change in the concept of mass. The use of "necessarily" here is not in the deductive sense, but in the sense that the attempt to change our system while preserving certain constraints does not leave us with very many options.

The momentum case is an example of the replacement of one concept by another which seems very logical, yet here too we have to explain what connects the two concepts. The description that seems most plausible to me involves the laws obeyed by the concept of momentum. When we first define momentum by a particular formula, it seems that this formula could not possibly be changed. We write the law as:

$$F = ma$$

and we know that it can be generalized as:

$$F = \frac{\mathrm{d}(mv)}{\mathrm{d}t}.$$

The importance of this law makes its connection with the concept of momentum extremely important as well, so that we identify the relativistic expression that has to be put into the above equation with this concept. Thus, even though there is a physical magnitude involved here rather than some mathematical function, we can still see the deep connection between the Newtonian and the relativistic concepts of momentum.

The general structure of the transition is simple. Certain problems arise in our system of knowledge as a result of empirical or theoretical discoveries. Sometimes we abandon one of our generalizations or premises, but on other occasions we react by changing our concepts. We perform such a change while taking care to preserve the general structure of our system. The concept that takes the place of the previous one within the structure is identified with the concept whose place it takes.[5] We could also say that the old concept is valid for short distances or low velocities, but we need a new concept for velocities that approach that of light. This new concept must coincide with the old one in the case of short distances and low velocities, but it provides a new extrapolation for great distances and high velocities.

References are structures

In the present section I will try to complete this picture by comparing it with Frege's third argument, as presented in chapter 2. As mentioned, Frege's conclusion against the possibility of expansions was based on the claim that the expansion of concepts fails to preserve the truth-value of the sentences in which they appear. From this viewpoint, we would have to give up the very idea of attributing reference to expressions and reject the extensionalist paradigm that associates references with linguistic expressions, with the enormous simplification this brings to logic. But the approach presented above allows us to avoid this conclusion as well, since we can see the reference of expressions as sensitive to the stage of the concept at which the expressions are used. Thus the reference of a sentence is no longer a simple truth-value that remains with it forever, but rather something that reflects the changes in the extension of the concepts in the sentence – that is, their stages. The reference of a sentence is thus a tree of truth-values.

For example, we can describe the "+" function as a tree of stages. At each of these stages we adopt the appropriate laws for defining the reference of all the other sentences and the expressions out of which these sentences are composed, so that the principle of compositionality is preserved: the reference of an expression is a function of the references of its components. Thus the sentence "Every quadratic equation has at least one square root" has one truth-value for the natural numbers and a different one for the complex numbers.

It is convenient to describe this situation in the Tarskian terms I used for the presentation of expansions above. Let us say that we have a model of a particular language in which the square root function is represented by a tree.[6] The original model gives rise to branches, leading to a tree of

---

[5] The reader is referred here to Putnam's criterion for distinguishing between conceptual change and "mere relabeling" in Putnam (1975b).

[6] For the moment we will ignore the nature of the expansion and the possibility of adding mathematical entities to the model; this possibility is discussed in the next chapter.

models. In each of the models the predicates are given an interpretation that fixes the references of the sentences in which they appear. Let us also say that the primitive names that denote objects (as opposed to definite descriptions and expressions like "$f(a)$") do not change their reference. Then the principle that the reference of a name is the object it denotes remains valid. The objects do not change, and this unchanging quality makes it possible to speak about the changes they do undergo, for if everything were to change there would not remain any "object" that could undergo changes.[7]

This removes the point from the third argument. The fact that a certain predicate $P(\quad)$ is undefined at a does not imply that two different predicates are involved, since they can well be two different stages of the same predicate. Similarly, the undefined status of the predicates mentioned in the second argument (from chapter 2) should not cause problems. Not only can we study partially defined concepts, but a full grasp of the logical form of concepts requires us to offer a notation that respects this type of concept. Now, this does not rule out arbitrary expansions of partially defined concepts for use in a specific task – as Frege does in the *Grundgesetze*. We only have to remember that this is a tentative expansion. Similarly, when we define an expression, thus giving it a name, we are obviously taking it upon ourselves to use this expression permanently with this meaning, but there is also an "as if" quality to this acceptance. We know that this acceptance is only valid for this particular stage of the concept.

In this view the definition of a function in parts looks different. Frege denounced the custom of mathematicians for defining functions in stages, leaving their ultimate meaning open. But Frege uses this pages-long denunciation, which is based on his arguments against expansions, in a critique of some remarks of Peano's. I will cite Frege's critique of Peano at this point in order to demonstrate how close Peano's view is to the one being developed here:

Thus, Peano says: "Frege requires one definition alone for every sign." And this is my opinion too, if it is a matter of a sign not containing variable letters. But if the definiendum contains variable letters, then so far as I can see, it is in general necessary to give conditional or hypothetical definitions of the expression and to give as many definitions as there are kinds of entities on which we perform

---

[7] Although the process of external expansion in which objects are added should not be forgotten. This is discussed below, in chapter 6. Even if these objects are forced on us, however, they do not undergo any change.

this operation. Thus the formula "$a + b$" will first be defined when a and b are integers, then a second time when they are fractions, then again when they are irrational or complex. It is met with again between two vectors, and will be defined over again; and so on. With the progress of science the meaning of this same formula is always being further extended. The various meanings of the symbol "$a + b$" have common properties; but these are insufficient to determine all the values that this expression can have (Frege 1977a, vol. II, footnote to sec. 57).

Frege cites Peano as having given in to the negligent practice of mathematicians of using the same symbol even though its meaning has changed. Instead, claims Frege, Peano should have first seen to it that the rigorous logical requirements were preserved, and only later adopted shortcuts to avoid complicated expressions. Frege insists that all terms should be defined once and for all, and not over and over again, as accepted by Peano. This demand is entirely justified, as the same expression cannot be given several meanings. Nevertheless, from the viewpoint described above, it is clear that Frege is not taking seriously a problem that Peano is well aware of. Even though Frege's notation for concepts satisfies a higher standard of rigorousness than Peano's, it seems that Peano was aware that functions can be expanded and was trying to express this property in his understanding of how functions should be defined. It is not negligence to accept the mathematical practice of continuing to use the same symbol after a concept has been expanded. Rather, a complete notation for what is involved in the definition of a function should be sensitive to the fundamentals of mathematical methodology, which includes the expansion of functions. Building on Peano's intuition here, it would be desirable for the constraints that guide us in expanding concepts to be expressed in the way we write our definitions. Our notation should include not only the concepts at a particular stage but also the system that forces their expansion, the nature and structure of this system, the result of the expansion, and the possibility that this may be a starting point for a new one. Such a notation, which was begun in $L(F)$ with formulas such as "$F(S, h(a) = b)$," might be even more complicated than Frege's, but this should not be seen as a reason to avoid it. Once we have a correct notation, however long it might be, we can always adopt laws and agreements for simplifying it.

Writing the logic of our language requires sensitivity to its open texture and the rational way it develops. Frege made the first step in this direction when he distinguished between predicates and proper names, between expressions with and without variables. Frege used the metaphor of being "unsaturated" to describe what he considered a property of some concepts – their need for an object or another concept with which to form a stable relation. This metaphor can also be used in another way. Our predicates and our knowledge about them are such that they tend to go beyond their boundaries. When we place them in one area of the world they try to force themselves on other areas. In mathematics, as we shall see later, they even form new areas entirely.

Definitions and family resemblance

I would like to broaden the discussion by commenting on Wittgenstein's use of expansions in mathematics to elucidate his view of the concept "game," which is such a central example of his general approach. According to the view of family resemblance, when a word refers to a collection of objects we should not search for one essence, one property that is common to all its applications. Instead we should expect to discover that some of its applications have one property in common while others have a different common property. When we look at all the things that are called "ice cream," for example, we find that we cannot include them all in one definition. Sometimes we use the expression for a sweet cold food made of milk, but if we do not force our hand by stipulating that this is the only proper use of the expression, we will see that it is sometimes made without milk, or without sugar, and that sometimes it can even be served hot. Despite this open texture, the expression cannot be expanded to include anything at all, as we cannot call hot, spicy bean soup "ice cream."

Wittgenstein finds this general characteristic in mathematics as well:

And for instance the kinds of number form a family in the same way. Why do we call something a "number"? Well, perhaps because it has a – direct – relationship with several things that have hitherto been called number; and this can be said to give it an indirect relationship to other things we call the same name. And we extend our concept of number as in spinning a thread we twist fibre on fibre. And the strength of the thread does not reside in the fact that some one fibre runs through its whole length, but in the overlapping of many fibres (Wittgenstein 1953, sec. 67).

The idea of concept stages is clearly similar to the notion of family resemblance. The laws that are preserved in the transition from one stage of a concept to another are Wittgenstein's "fibres." The problem is in Wittgenstein's comments on this issue, his appealing to this similarity to claim that even in the mathematical case concepts do not have a unique essence, and therefore he sees no necessity for defining the concept of a game. I do not intend to discuss Wittgenstein's claim that the concept of a game cannot be defined; however, I shall argue that this claim cannot be inferred from the analysis of *mathematical* expansions of concepts.

In order to understand this last claim, consider one difference between the idea that concepts have stages and Wittgenstein's notion of family resemblance. The notion of stages leads to a tree structure that does not exist in the case of family resemblance. A tree structure implies not only that all the stages have a common root, but also directionality. There is a particular point at which we move from one stage to the next, and all the stages have to satisfy certain laws. Higher branches of the tree are dependent on lower ones in the sense that the lower ones partially determine the meaning of the upper ones. This makes the metaphor of the tree even more apt, since one can say that the more advanced stages derive their sustenance from the previous ones, but not the other way around.

This important distinction challenges Wittgenstein's use of the expansion of the concept of number to obviate the necessity of defining the word "game." First, even if we agree that there is no common essence to all numbers, this does not imply that definitions are non-essential. On the contrary, a necessary condition for the process of expansion of the sort that occurs in mathematics is the existence of definitions that are then superseded. Second, it may even be said that each expansion brings us closer to the essence of the concept which we have hitherto grasped only partially.

In trying to obviate the necessity for definitions, Wittgenstein should avoid using the example of expansions in mathematics. He should rather discuss words like "game" by highlighting the fact that these are *not* words used in mathematics. Wittgenstein sees changes in mathematical definition as being similar to changes in the rules of games like chess, and so he discusses the mathematical case in the light of his views about chess. He thus makes covert use of his views about chess in his analysis of concept changes in mathematics. As a result, he is not only using the mathematical example to elucidate his views about games and language, but is also using these views to color the mathematical example.[8]

Let us try to formulate a different picture of definitions which will

---

[8] The parallel move reappears in his theory that proofs modify concepts (see the second part of chapter 8).

take into account non-arbitrary expansions as well. When we admit the existence of concept stages we are not obviating the importance of definitions in mathematics, but are rather suggesting a different theory of definitions in this field. The phenomenon of expansions does not necessitate viewing the attempt to find a common essence for all numbers as an illusion based on a mistake. On the contrary, we are obliged to continue searching for essences and definitions, even though we must remember that we have to do this differently. Actually, expansions can give us a deeper understanding of the essence of a function; at least this has happened in many cases. For example, after the sine and cosine functions were defined for the angles of a right triangle, they were expanded to all real numbers (and then to complex numbers as well). The interest generated by this expansion encouraged mathematicians to search for equations that would force the expansion, and these equations later served to define the sine and cosine functions. Only the properties that can determine the expansion of a function and are preserved in it can be said to be the essence of the function. At the end of such a process the definition we began with is changed, and we now perceive the earlier definition as having been merely temporary. Thanks to the expansion we have now obtained a better definition of the function. In chapter 7 I discuss the view of Gödel, who went even further in this direction.

If a discovery of the "essence" of a concept had to be permanent, and totally obviated any sort of incomplete definition process, as Frege believed, then Wittgenstein would be right in inferring that since this "essence" can undergo changes there cannot be any real essence at all. But I am rejecting the Fregean view, traces of which can still be seen in Wittgenstein's notion of family resemblance.

TWO NON-FREGEAN VIEWS

The suggested distinction between a concept and a concept stage is essentially faithful to Frege. Predicates still denote concepts, and all concepts have an extension, even though this extension is now complex and the concepts are no longer variables. We can take this view even further, placing the concept stages in some Platonic universe, as if the tree and its stages were all engraved there and the expansions were paths in that universe. These are thus the minimal changes that Frege would have to make if he were willing to accept the notion of concept change.

It is also possible, however, to fit the idea of forced expansions into a non-realist position. I will therefore suggest two refinements of the picture put forward above which are sensitive to requirements that are generally not met by realist positions. I will begin with the weaker refinement.

There are no concepts

The view proposed above is that concepts can be described as trees of stages, where the most important facet of this picture is the equivalence relation "A is a stage of the same concept as B." It is possible, however, to avoid reifying the collection of elements that obey this equivalence relation and calling it a tree, remaining rather with the concept stages alone. We could then say that we do not grasp the extension of a concept, but are connected only with its stages. This lack of access to the concept itself can be justified in a number of ways. One consideration is that the extension of the entire tree is too large, and so it cannot be seen as one object among many.[9] It may also be possible to use Occam's razor to abolish the idea of a concept. It seems to me sufficient for our purposes to use the idea of concept stages and the relation "A and B are stages of the same concept." After there has been some development we may say from this later viewpoint that different stages of the same concept are involved.

Another, more important, reason for refusing to accept expansions of concepts and making do with concept stages alone is based on a qualitative problem. We have no access to what may develop out of the concept stage in our possession at the present time, and we cannot even imagine all the different ways in which it might be possible to develop the concept. When a concept stage is expanded to the next stage, deep changes in understanding are needed, as well as various considerations that we have no way of claiming we now possess. Requiring a connection with everything that might develop from a given concept stage entails a viewpoint of eternity, and it is not clear what such a thing might be. I did indeed try to avoid this problem by distinguishing between grasping a concept stage and being connected to a concept, but I am now suggesting that this alone might not be enough to solve the problem.

This way of eliminating concepts is of interest because it gives us a way to express the degrees of freedom in the transition from one concept stage to another, as is done in non-mathematical settings. When we

---

[9] The distinction between proper classes and sets that is made in set theory in response to the paradoxes discovered in that theory supports this consideration. See, e.g., Dummett (1973, pp. 532–3).

realize that concepts change without our having full control over them, but rather that these changes are dependent to a great extent on culture and contingencies (or, as a Foucault follower might say, on the system that controls the society's language), which cannot be predicted before they occur, then we cannot say that we grasp them fully.

Consider, for example, the expansion of disease terminology to include insanity. This sort of expansion is not forced in the sense of being fully derived from the situation prior to the expansion, and it may sometimes be determined by purely pragmatic considerations. Even now, when the diagnoses of some mental diseases may change, we cannot claim that these changes are determined, even if we agree that they are not merely random either. In light of this fact, it is not clear how we could think of the full tree of the extension of the concept of disease, with all its transformations, as having existed from the time the word "disease" was first used.

When the motivation for the expansion of the concept is ideological rather than scientific, then it is difficult to speak of a concept stage. A good example of this difference is the distinction between the scientific definition of "milk" and the definition given by Jewish law, or halakha, which are seen today as two different definitions. In the view of modern chemistry, anything with the same chemical structure as milk is considered to be milk. A rabbi versed in Jewish law, however, might well claim that only a substance that was actually extracted from a lactating animal can be considered milk, with all the halakhic restrictions this entails, whereas a chemical identical to milk that was not obtained from an animal may be considered non-dairy for halakhic purposes. In such a case we are confronted with two different concepts of milk. Let us then try to place ourselves in the shoes of an Israelite of the First Temple period, nearly three millennia ago, who does not have even the faintest notion that there could be developments in the concept of milk. Whether or not he could be said to grasp the concept of milk is thus dependent on subsequent developments in science and halakha, none of which he could possibly foresee. We therefore cannot say that he grasped the entire concept of milk with all its branchings, even if the present-day chemical and halakhic concepts of milk are not random or arbitrary developments of the biblical concept.

Concepts as expandable sets

The second refinement is based on questions about the boundaries between the various concept stages. Where does one stage end and the next one begin? Is the division between two stages of a concept a sharp one? Could what appears to us as one stage actually be composed of several stages? Is it possible that every application of a concept is actually an expansion of the concept?

These questions arise even for arithmetic. In this case there are the questions of how we know that all the numbers belong to one stage, and what makes us think that all atomic sentences of arithmetic are grasped in the same way, without any differences. Wittgenstein, for example, suggested that propositions about very large numbers may be an expansion of the propositions we actually use. When we say that 2^{100} is greater than 2^{99}, he claims, we are actually forcing an expansion, and not merely asserting it on the basis of definitions that were always in our field of meaning. This position has a clear motivation, since we have no connection with these numbers except through descriptions of them using certain functions. We do not decide that 2^{101} is greater than 2^{100} on the basis of computation; rather, we make use of a principle that is true of powers and expand it to expressions such as 2^{100} or 2^{101}.

This position is especially apt for arithmetic, as the transition from smaller numbers that we can easily grasp to larger numbers that we find difficult to imagine can be described similarly to the transition from the natural numbers to the integers. There is no formal difficulty in describing the whole set of atomic truths of arithmetic as the result of a forced expansion that begins with the first hundred natural numbers. The identities that are true in the case of the numbers we can easily grasp are extended to larger numbers, and such expansions can even be seen as composed of two processes. We can say that what seems to be the computation of "$2^{101} > 2^{100}$" is only apparently a computation, and what we are actually doing is expanding the number system to include expressions such as "2^{101}", just as it will later be expanded to include "the square root of -1."

This position has an obvious advantage in that what I am calling the "transition from one concept stage to another" is not a different kind of operation from that which creates what I call a stage. Peacock's principle is already active at the level of the natural numbers,[10] leading to an

---

[10] Another advantage of this position is its epistemic value. Hilbert's program suggested seeing mathematical knowledge as composed of two parts, an intuitive part and an ideal part, with the second constructed on the basis of the first. This position makes it possible to deal with complex expressions like 2^{101} on the basis of the limited part consisting of the first hundred natural numbers. In other words, we expand the set of ideal sentences to expressions that we have no intuitive access to, even though they do not include quantifiers or identities that refer to an infinite number of values.

intensionalist view of concepts, as the extension of even a single concept stage is influenced by laws of expansion that we were not aware of. The extension of a concept is thus subject to a process that is essentially based on the logical connections found in expansions. The notion of a concept thus acquires a new meaning: a means of determining extension through non-arbitrary expansions. Grasping a concept is thus knowing how to determine or even create a particular extension.

The problem with this exotic view, however, is how to characterize the difference between "$2^0 = 1$" and "$2^{101} > 2^{100}$." "2^0" appears to be outside the boundaries of our original definition of the power function, while "2^{101}" is clearly part of the definition of the power expansion (by mathematical induction). The first is meaningless until we define it, while the second represents an operation that we know how to perform in order to find the number that satisfies it, even if this process might take more time than we have at our disposal. When the laws of the power function were first established, it was clear that they are true of all the natural numbers, but it was not clear that they are true for the zero as well until we extended the laws to cover this case. We would have to say that we merely feel that there are two different types of processes involved, or that the difference can be seen as that between two kinds of expansions.

I am therefore unsure that this view can be defended. Perhaps we should claim that the difference between "$2^0 = 1$" and "$2^{101} > 2^{100}$" is a matter of degree: every new computation is an expansion, but only when we encounter some obstacle – because there is a contradiction to a law we consider valid, or because the expansion simply seems wrong – do we become aware of the fact that we are actually performing an expansion. Here we can consider the problems associated with the expression "this case was already included in the cases I meant," making use of Kripke's remarks about Wittgenstein's "skeptical" analysis. Although we have the feeling that the latter case was already defined, this feeling plays no role in our understanding of the power function or our ability to calculate all sorts of expressions in which the power symbol appears. In any case, even if we can defend this view, it still remains to show why it is a convincing stance and how it competes with other alternatives. Certainly it has the advantage of showing that functions such as powers may be accessible to us, but this can be accounted for by a different approach. I therefore leave the issue at this point, in the hope that further study of expansions may offer new constraints to help us decide the matter.

In sum, this chapter has developed a view of the relation between a concept and its extension that was necessitated by the previous discussion

of forced expansions. I have presented a picture which I then sharpened by examining Frege's objections from chapter 2, moving gradually
to Wittgenstein's view of definitions in his discussion of family resemblance, and then to the much-discussed subjects of conceptual changes
or changes in the meanings of our words. Finally I strengthened the proposed view by developing it in non-Fregean directions. A careful study is
required in order to cover this schematic direction with flesh and blood.

APPENDIX: A SHORT DISCUSSION WITH LAKATOS

The thinker who is most closely identified with the notion of conceptual change in mathematics is Imre Lakatos, who presented his ideas in
his seminal work, *Proofs and Refutations: The Logic of Mathematical Discovery*
(Lakatos 1976). It is therefore important to discuss the relevance of what
I have been presenting here to Lakatos's thought. To be sure, I cannot
discuss this issue exhaustively, but I will offer some general remarks pertaining to essential points in Lakatos's position.

Lakatos showed how concepts develop hand in hand with the processes
of proof and refutation that are so central to mathematical methodology.
The range of a concept is determined through the attempt to prove
our hypotheses. As we try to make the proof more rigorous, as general
as possible yet also immune to counterexamples, we are determining
the range of the concept as well. Lakatos illustrated the complexity of
this process with the case of an informal proof of Euler's theorem on
polyhedra. Nevertheless, he scarcely touched upon the problems in the
philosophy of language, the analysis of sentences, and the relation of this
analysis to the world. There is one exceptional remark of his, however,
that expresses a recommendation to discuss such problems and thus ties
Lakatos's ideas with the ones I present in my discussion of Gödel in
chapter 7:

> As far as naive classification is concerned, nominalists are close to the truth
> when claiming that the only thing that polyhedra have in common is their name.
> But after a few centuries of proofs and refutations, as the theory of polyhedra
> develops, and theoretical classification replaces naive classification, the balance
> changes in favour of the realist. The problem of the universals ought to be
> reconsidered in view of the fact that, as knowledge grows, language changes
> (Lakatos 1976, p. 92n).

This remark is not at all trivial, showing clearly that Lakatos
does not accept Kuhn's assertion that changes in concepts lead to

incommensurability; on the contrary, Lakatos insists that our language must change as a *result* of the growth of our knowledge. I therefore believe that the present discussion may well complement Lakatos's position, supporting it from the aspect of the philosophy of language.[11] Without such support, a follower of Frege could dismiss Lakatos's view as unimportant. I shall discuss this issue shortly.

I will now present two examples of the usefulness of Lakatos's discussion for the theory of expansions and the various ways of analyzing it. So far I have been discussing forced expansions as the attempt to determine how to apply our rules to a new, undefined area. In the case of the polyhedra, however, Lakatos's idea of "monster barring" presents the opposite problem. Sometimes we have to limit the range of a concept in order to preserve an elegant proof. If we allow the concept to extend over one range we will not be able to use the proof, while a slight restriction of the range will allow us to keep our informal proof. Could this be considered the non-arbitrary restriction of a concept, forming a mirror image of nonarbitrary expansion? In order to deal with this question we would have somehow to formalize the informal proofs or hypotheses, thus deviating to some extent from Lakatos's intentions. But if we do not mind doing so, we can use his discussion to derive some ideas that may be interesting from the viewpoint of logic.

Lakatos also suggests a bolder move, which is in a certain sense the opposite of the approach that I have been presenting. He says that true research in mathematics may include attempts to refute the proofs we propose by expanding our concepts. In other words, we do not expand our concepts in order to preserve the laws of mathematics, as I have been suggesting, but rather in order to refute mathematical proofs and the laws we used in formulating them. Lakatos illustrates this proposal with the example of the polyhedra. This raises the question of whether his suggestion, which seems at first glance to be exactly the opposite of mine, could actually be complementary to it.

Here, however, I would like to consider a more important issue, namely, the conflict between Lakatos's position and that of Frege. At issue is the place of formal logic and its contribution to understanding mathematics. Frege and his followers believe that the key to understanding mathematics and mathematical proofs, as well as human language, is the use of logical research similar to that of Frege. Lakatos, in contrast,

---

[11] I wish to thank Joseph Agassi, a student and colleague of Lakatos, for the encouragement he gave me at an early stage of developing the ideas in this book, and for notifying me of the possible contribution of the ideas proposed here for a Lakatosian.

believes that such research is mere formalism, reminding the logicians of the importance of informal proofs and their place in the creation of mathematics. What I would like to discuss here is how this controversy can be understood in the light of my suggestions about expansions.

At first glance there seems to be a deep conflict between Lakatos and Frege, as can be seen in the following quotation from Lakatos:

> The history of mathematics and the logic of mathematical discovery, i.e., the phylogenesis and the ontogenesis of mathematical thought, cannot be developed without the criticism and ultimate rejection of formalism (Lakatos 1976, p. 4).

Moreover, in spite of the view he presented in the above passage, Lakatos was not against all formalism. This can be seen when we consider the period in which he was writing. He had taken upon himself to warn the philosophers of science against a naive attitude towards formalism, claiming that formalist meta-mathematics cannot give a true picture of mathematical methodology. But I do not think that Lakatos drew an antiformalist conclusion from this. Formalism is one stage in the development of mathematical knowledge, a stage that is important to the process of turning informal proofs into rigorous ones.[12] In addition, it is possible to read Lakatos as saying that our concepts are shaped in the process of making our proofs more exact, which constitutes a condition for proper formalization. After this formalization is achieved, another process may develop that will lead us back to natural language, followed by yet another formalization process, and so on. All this shows that formalism is an essential stage in understanding the methodology of mathematics.

At this point it is possible to suggest a new idea arising from the last passage of Lakatos quoted above. In his honor I present this discussion as a dialogue.

EXPANSION ADVOCATE: What do you two think about the fact that you seem to agree that logic cannot treat mathematics dynamically? You, Frege, claim that logic has no connection with history, while you, Lakatos, agree that a logic worthy of the name requires defined concepts that never change.

LAKATOS: Actually, I am not so happy to be in the same camp as Frege and logicians of his sort, since our agreement is only an illusion. Remember

---

[12] See his paper "What does a mathematical proof prove?" (written between 1959 and 1961) in Lakatos (1978), pp. 61–70.

that my book is called *Proofs and Refutations: The Logic of Mathematical Discovery*. Although I reject the usefulness of formalist research into the development of mathematical knowledge, I nevertheless call what I do "logic." Perhaps you did not notice that in the end I suggest that logic is a reflection on mathematical dialogues and the genealogy of mathematics, the way I do it.

FREGE: I too am not happy to be in the company of someone who has ruined logic under the pretext of a logical investigation. My view is that logic is the study of truth and valid arguments. What Lakatos studies is a sort of broad heuristics – the rationale of mathematical discovery. Lakatos is actually suggesting a psychology or anthropology of mathematical research. There's no harm in doing this, of course, but please don't call it logic!

EXPANSION ADVOCATE: Let's not argue about the name of the discipline, and let's avoid calling each other names as well. From your viewpoint, Frege, everyone calls something else "logic" and claims that they are doing a logical investigation, apparently because this discipline has such a good reputation. If this is the case, then there isn't even any argument between the two of you, but you, Lakatos, seem to believe that there really is a controversy.

LAKATOS: That's right. We actually belong to two different camps that have always existed in philosophy. There have always been philosophers who believed that logic is the study of thought and assertions. They examine and analyze thought, and they also tend towards Platonism, considering thoughts to constitute a third realm. Other philosophers consider dialogue to be the most important unit for analysis. (And then, of course, there are those who combine the two, such as Plato himself.) For the first group it is merely incidental that thoughts are asserted by subjects; what is important about them is whether they actually express the truth they are meant to express. For the second group, to which I myself belong, it is dialogue that is primary. What is important is the description of how truth develops through dialogue, and the way people come to agree or disagree.

EXPANSION ADVOCATE: But why do you think that what Frege is doing is not essential for the analysis of dialogue? I may be mistaken, but don't you see agreement as replacing objective truth? It is not because both sides have reached an agreement that they believe they have achieved the truth. On the contrary, it is because they have exhausted the debate and reached the truth that they suggest coming to an agreement.

LAKATOS: I am not a conventionalist!

EXPANSION ADVOCATE: I suppose that each of you considers himself the representative of one camp in the history of philosophy, and this clearly makes the debate between you more dramatic. It seems to me that if you would agree to give up the dramatic quality of the differences between you, you might be able to achieve an interesting dialogue.

FREGE AND LAKATOS: We are willing to give it a chance.

EXPANSION ADVOCATE: I believe that you, Lakatos, have not refuted the elegant laws that you, Frege, have described so intelligently. Yet you have to admit that what Lakatos is doing is not merely describing tricks for finding out mathematical truths, nor is it merely the history of mathematics in the sense of who discovered what. When Lakatos describes the sequence of events that led to the concept of uniform convergence (in Lakatos 1976, pp. 127–41), he is helping us understand the point of the concept, as well as the concept itself. Now when you, Frege, described proofs you thought that the concepts in a proof could not undergo any changes, and in this respect you were right, but when you, Lakatos, described the dynamics that create a concept, you committed yourself to leaving concepts open, with changeable boundaries. Each of you had to accept a particular view of concepts in order to describe what you were interested in. Thus, if we want to preserve Frege's approach we will have to keep concepts bound, while if we choose to follow in Lakatos's direction we will have to leave them open. What do you think of the description so far?

FREGE AND LAKATOS: We are waiting to hear your own suggestion. We hope you won't make it too complicated.

EXPANSION ADVOCATE: Thank you for your willingness to listen. It seems to me that even though each of you has reached different conclusions about concepts and their extensions, it would not be philosophically appropriate, or at least not elegant, to say that you have completely independent notions on the relation between them. Instead, it would be much better to try to find a single theory on this issue.

FREGE AND LAKATOS: Let's hear what you have to say.

EXPANSION ADVOCATE: What would you think about saying that there are two different types of stages? In one type the concept is fixed, since it cannot change in the process of a proof. This is the stage that Frege analyzes, and that Lakatos calls "formalistic." In the other type of stage the concept can undergo a dynamic process, and at those times Frege's strict requirements cannot be applied to it.

FREGE AND LAKATOS: Continue, we need to hear more.

EXPANSION ADVOCATE: I would therefore say that, on the one hand, you, Frege, are mistaken in saying that the investigation of deduction is the only constraint on an analysis of concepts, and you only saw part of the issue. On the other hand, you, Lakatos, have not been careful enough about a different aspect of the issue. If you will allow me, I believe that I can explain what you can learn from Frege.

LAKATOS: This is beginning to sound interesting.

EXPANSION ADVOCATE: The second stage, which should be your domain, seems to be one that uses natural language, in which concepts are supposed to be open. But I don't understand why you limit the formal stage to the investigation of deduction. What you call formalism can help us understand what is happening in the second stage as well!

LAKATOS: How so?

EXPANSION ADVOCATE: Just look, and you'll see that all the research on the development of concepts has been done with tools derived from Frege's work. Even though I am very sympathetic towards your position, Lakatos, what has been suggested in this book is closer in spirit to Frege than to you.

LAKATOS: I think you're going too far. I don't think your analysis of expansions is very useful, since it only captures certain aspects of the development of mathematical concepts.

EXPANSION ADVOCATE: That's true, but look what it does capture! It helps us better understand the development of the concept of number and the relation between expansions and deductions. It has given us tools to describe controversies in the history of mathematics, and it has shown that there are different concepts of expansions. And what should be particularly interesting to you, Lakatos, is that it has also created a space of new questions. There is also another important point which points to a possible dialogue between your position and what you call "formalism."

LAKATOS: Please explain.

EXPANSION ADVOCATE: I believe that the notion of conceptual expansion should be treated the way you have treated the concept of polyhedra. I might add that I had to go through an extensive process of trial and error before I arrived at the concept of expansion I have presented here. What I am now suggesting is that your discussion of polyhedra could be considered the start of the discussion of the idea of stretching concepts.

LAKATOS: Could you expand on this notion?

EXPANSION ADVOCATE: You discuss the idea of the counterexample, the attempt to preserve informal proofs, limiting the extension of concepts, while avoiding arbitrary limitations and similar notions. In the process you not only explain the term "polyhedra" and the different senses this term has been given in the process of proving and refuting theorems about it, but you also discuss the changes undergone in our very understanding of the notion of counterexamples, expansions of concepts, and the like. Towards the end of the first chapter of your book you yourself noticed this when you began to consider the limitations of the process of expansion, especially when you were discussing a case in which you believed that the notion of expansion itself had been expanded incautiously.

LAKATOS: That's right. You see yourself that I thought about the issue long before you suggested it.

EXPANSION ADVOCATE: What I am suggesting is that you should use my present proposal to amend your own notion of expansions. The analogy with the case of polyhedra is meant to help me explain my intention. When you investigated the polyhedra you did not do this is a void – you had Euler's informal proof that guided you in your discussion. Without Euler's proof you might not have thought of asking whether some odd shapes are actually polyhedra.[13] A similar thing occurs in the case of expansions. We

---

[13] A confirmation to this may be found in the above note on the debate between nominalists and realists.

now have some theorems about expansions, and attempting to produce
new ones can help us further our understanding of concepts and how they
are expanded.

LAKATOS: I am beginning to understand what you are saying, but I hope you
will agree that, just as in the case of ordinary mathematical concepts, we
should not believe that the only thing we need is the formal analysis you
have offered. Moreover, your analysis relies on the notion of a function,
which is itself the product of a process of increasing expansion that you
accept as obvious.

EXPANSION ADVOCATE: I accept your comment that I assumed a concept
of the function, as it would be rather difficult to analyze the concept of
the function using that very concept. I also assumed the truth of classical
logic, even though, in Brouwer's view, it too is the product of an incautious
expansion. In general, Tarski's notion of a model, which I have been using
here, is a generalization – namely, of the concept of algebraic structure –
which I have not analyzed here either, and which I may not be able to
analyze at all. It can be said, as a rule, that it is unwise to pretend to be able
to analyze the phenomenon of expansions absolutely. It would be better to
create perspectives on natural language in the form of general calculi, and
then to investigate whether expansions can be described in such a theory.

In the end, the participants in this dialogue agreed that this was merely
the start of a discussion that would have to be continued at a later date.

CHAPTER 6

From words to objects

So far I have discussed expansions of concepts that do not involve
the addition of new objects. Now I will examine whether it is possible to generalize this discussion to external expansions, where new
objects are involved. The point I suggest here is basically a formalist one, claiming that words such as "-3" and "$\sqrt{(-1)}$" can play a
crucial role in external expansions, but this approach is given a new
sense here: the important external expansions such as negative and
complex numbers are viewed as the result of stretching the identity
relation. I shall then move to the debate between Frege and the formalists, trying to find a way to retain the intuitions of both sides.
Corresponding to the transition from words to objects that occurs
in external expansions, there is a subtler transition in which constraints on potential entities are transformed into axioms on a well-
defined realm of objects. This is the subject of the third section of this
chapter.

This leaves us with the question of where to start. Do we assume,
like Kronecker, that the natural numbers are at the basis of all expansions of numbers? It seems to me that this assumption is not necessary. One way that we can begin, which is probably not the only
possible way, is to construct the ordinal numbers and the relations
between them, hoping that further expansions will take us to richer
structures. The appendix to this chapter suggests one such approach
to the construction of the ordinal numbers, seeing them as an expansion of the language of the predicate calculus, which is needed
for the use of logical laws such as existential instantiation (EI). This
move is intended to obviate the need to use the concept of structure,
while making use of an insight of Benacerraf on the nature of the
numbers.

EXPANDING THE IDENTITY

When we expand a particular function we allow a combination of signs that was previously meaningless to denote some object. "2^{-3}" is an expression that at one time did not denote any object, but when we examined the space of objects known to us, we came to the conclusion that identifying this expression with $\frac{1}{8}$ is the best possible use for it. This is so because the laws for working with powers seem to lead directly to the identity of "2^{-3}" with $\frac{1}{8}$. In this way the power function with which we began is expanded and becomes applicable to the *object* -3 and not only the *sign* "-3". We can therefore say that if the object -3 were given some description, say S, then the complex sign "2^{S}" would have to denote $\frac{1}{8}$ as well.

The next question is what happens when there is no object for the meaningless sign to denote. This question arose in cases such as the expression "$2-7$" or "the square root of -1". I suggest that in this case the parallel move in the world of reference is the creation or constitution of a new object. Such a move takes us from words to objects. The suggestion just offered shows how forced internal and external expansions are profoundly interconnected. External expansions are those expansions where it "just happens" that there is no appropriate object. Since internal expansions are more general and occur in other sciences as well, we can understand the genealogy of mathematical objects better in light of this more general type of operation.

This comment is aimed at the various ways of accounting for the phenomenon of expansions in mathematics. We have accounts that are based on concepts from algebra, the most famous of which is the algebraic extension of fields. In order to describe such expansions, we start with some field, e.g. $\mathbb{R}$ or $\mathbb{Q}$, and describe the expansion as the addition of a root for some polynomial over the field which has no roots in the field. This algebraic concept of expansions was generalized using the terms of model theory, and it boils down to a situation where we have a set of sentences of the form $\exists x(\Phi(x))$, which are false in model $\boldsymbol{M}$, where the set Σ of sentences is true. We try to find a model where Σ *and* all sentences of the form $\exists x(\Phi(x))$ in the set are true. Indeed, using the notion of algebraic closure and Robinson's notion of model completeness we can describe certain expansions of mathematical objects as the closure of structures in which we are required to preserve all the laws (of the form $\forall x(\Psi(x))$ that were true in the original model.

This shows us that we can relate the narrative of mathematical objects in different ways, with each story having its own merits. The advantage of the account presented here is, as we said, that it links external and internal expansions. Moreover, our account naturally suggests the possibility of forced expansions which are not strongly forced (as is the case with the field of P-adic numbers or infinite numbers), since we are not required to preserve the field axioms, nor do we need to keep all generalizations Σ, as we must with algebraic expansions or other existing closure expansions. Generally, we see such situations as the action of a model $\boldsymbol{M}$ and a set of sentences $\boldsymbol{T}$ on expressions of the type "$F(a)$" (e.g., "$\sqrt{(-1)}$"), where performing the expansion provides a reference for such expressions.

Due to the connection between external and internal expansions, we can generalize our claims about internal expansions to the case of external expansions as well, and consider the creation of objects as stemming from expansions of the identity relation. This relation too consists of stages, except that in this case the transition from one stage to the next also involves the addition of new objects. The expansion of the identity relation is thus also an expansion of the possible values of variables which require an equality condition on what can be substituted for them. Such expansions are thus an expansion of what exists.

The transition from a set of non-arbitrary identities to entities may be called reification, but we can also view it from another perspective. For every entity, all its predicates are usually determined. A reified entity comes into being when we perform the converse operation: if by non-arbitrary expansions we can decide the truth-values of all sentences in which an expression (such as "$\sqrt{(-1)}$" or perhaps even "the set of natural numbers") appears, then we are allowed to expand our ontology by admitting a new non-arbitrary object.[1] The relation between such non-arbitrary objects and the set of original objects is analogous to the relation between the power function after its expansion to complex numbers and the original function.

A problem arises, however, as the expansion of the identity relation cannot be either an internal or an external expansion. If it were an internal expansion, this would mean that the required object already exists, in which case no identity relation was expanded. And if it were an

---

[1] What if we cannot determine by non-arbitrary expansion the truth-value of certain sentences that contain these expressions? Should we open up a new category of, say, "partial objects"? I cannot discuss this here.

external expansion then we would be adding new objects that already satisfy identity relations.

Expanding the equality relation is thus different from other expansions of functions. The suggestion in mathematics is that adding mathematical objects is an expansion of equations, and that the mathematical objects are constituted by this expansion. There is thus a two-step process here. First certain equations are forced, and then the nominal expressions in these equations are reified in an expansion of the range of values that the variable can obtain.

A similar idea can be found in Peano's writings:

The same happens for the formula $a = b$. In some cases its meaning can be assumed as a primitive idea, in others it is defined; and precisely in arithmetic, given the equality of whole numbers, equality is defined between rationals, between irrationals, between imaginary numbers, etc. ... With the progress of science, the need is more and more felt to extend the meaning of the expression $a = b$. The various meanings have common properties, but I do not see how they suffice to determine all the possible meanings of equality (quoted in a footnote in Frege 1977a, vol. II, sec. 58).

If we combine this citation with the remark of Peano's cited in chapter 5, we can see that Peano associates expansions of functions with expansions of identity, discussing them in the same way. However, the idea of concept stages and the claim that the operation of expansion can be systematized allow us to answer Frege's criticism that Peano's suggestion is "monstrous" (ibid.). It was difficult for Peano to explain how to tie together all the meanings of equality, but the suggestions in the present book allow us to offer an answer by expanding the terminology of concept stages to the identity symbol. Thus, it is not necessary to assume that an ultimate meaning of the identity sign can be given once and for all. Just as there are stages in the development of the addition function, so there are stages of the equality function. In Peano's view, it is important not to define them in ways that would make their meaning closed to all further development. The present view thus provides a way of explaining Peano's position, so that it is not necessary to see it the way Frege did, as giving in to mathematicians' desire for convenience at the expense of a proper description of the logic of such expressions.

FREGE AND THE FORMALISTS

This description sheds a new light on the debate between the realist Frege, who rejected expansions of the numbers in the same way as expansions of concepts, and the formalist Hankel, who believed that the only thing that we have to be careful about in performing expansions is the consistency of the new system. One of Frege's criticisms of formalism can be used to explain the position presented above. Frege argued that we can only name objects which we know to exist. The names must come after the objects, not before them. But in the present case we can answer that we can impose certain formal identities before we know if there is an object to which the names in the identity relation refer. These would be a sort of potential identity.

Just as a Kantian may argue that objects are not some Aristotelian substance but categories of the understanding that allow us to tie together different images into an objective unity and turn them into "instances of the same object," so we too can argue that if we have a way of determining when a particular expression is equal to other expressions and when it is different from them – that is, when we can determine the truth-value of a family of equations – then we have an object. Stretching the truth to cover identities is thus a way of constituting objects.[2] Formalists can therefore consider their position strengthened, claiming that the negative numbers are not merely a consistent, interesting symbolic game but a "game" that arises naturally from the natural numbers. Thus the non-arbitrariness, or the reality, of numbers is not due to the fact that we have not yet found any contradiction in the system, but rather to the fact that the identities that preceded these objects arose out of the natural numbers in a forced way.

The above analysis also enables us to solve a problem that Frege pointed out in the formalist position. Frege tried to show that this position is absurd by arguing that if all we have to do in order to create expansions is add an object that has any property, then why not add an object that satisfies $x + 1 = x + 7$ (Frege 1980, sec. 96)?

Indeed, it cannot be argued against Frege that there are obviously no such numbers, since the analogy with external expansions shows us that a similar situation served as a reason for expanding the number system in the cases of adding the negative and the complex numbers. Frege could clearly insist that if we do not accept realism, then how can we know which description is legitimate and which one is not? After all, it

---

[2] Dummett (1973, p. 499) claims that Frege's context principle for reference interferes with his realism; the references of expressions that denote the names appearing in particular sentences are determined as soon as the sentences are given a truth-value. Mark Wilson (1992) claimed that the context principle emerges from the discussions of ideal objects in projective geometry, which Frege was aware of. With this interpretation the gap between formalism and realism can be narrowed significantly.

is well known that Frege considered mathematicians to be discoverers rather then people who simply create objects according to their fancies. He insisted that mathematicians are no different from geographers, who first discover new continents and only then give them a name. Therefore, Frege argues, it is wrong for formalists to try to create objects through expansions.

My answer to Frege is as follows. There are expressions which have no reference at a particular stage, but they are not merely empty names, since they have the form of a description. We can provide identity conditions for sentences containing these expressions by determining which laws we want to preserve in our expansions. Thus we are not obligated to formulate the identity conditions for any two complex numbers in advance. We can reach a situation in which one complex number is different from another by forcing them to be different. For example, the incorrectness of the identity $2i + 3 = 4 + 5i$, like the correctness of the identity $(2 + i) + i = (3 - 1) + 2i$, stems from the requirements we want to preserve. Similarly, the method of determining the identities between the numbers of elements in sets by one-to-one correspondence, which Frege uses in his *Foundations of Arithmetic* to construct the number system, is also a forced expansion. Had Frege chosen another law when he tried to impose identities between the numbers of elements in sets, he would have obtained a different number system.

Now if we are given the expression "$2 - 7$" we know very well that it cannot be equal to one of the natural numbers. If we want to preserve some of the laws for the natural numbers, then we know "$2 - 7$" must be different from the object that will be called "$1 - 100$." Similarly, we can ask how to add or subtract two vectors and which vectors are equal to each other, even if we do not know very much about vectors except for the fact that we want to construct a system for quantities that have a direction. After we determine which vectors are equal to one another, we can expand the addition and multiplication functions to cover them. But this is precisely the operation of determining the truth-values of new sentences. At the end of the process we will obtain the sentence "$(-2) \times (-2) = 4$" and all the other identities involving the new numbers (this issue is discussed further below).

But if we consider the "object" with the property "$x + 1 = x + 2$," we can give it a name, say "g," but we cannot impose any identities that could connect "g" with other numerals. In cases of this sort we discover that the attempt to preserve certain laws leads us to a dead end, which puts paid to this "game." The answer to Frege's question, then, is that as long as we do not know what system of constraints such a hypothetical object is supposed to obey, we do not have an unambiguous question. As soon as the appropriate constraints are decided upon – and we already know what the usual constraints are – then we reject the possibility of this sort of expansion, and we have an unambiguous answer to the question.

Frege thought that logic begins only when we have a well-defined system. Since the transition from one system to another does not involve logic, our considerations in expanding the number system, say to include the complex numbers, may belong to what is often called the context of discovery. In Frege's view, only once we have such a new system can we present it systematically and use logic to operate within it. But the viewpoint presented here looks at the issue differently. If we consider logic to be the investigation of truth, then it must be applied not only to objects that have already been constructed but also to the act of constructing them.

FROM CONSTRAINTS TO AXIOMS

I would like to discuss more fully one important move involved in this act of construction, illustrating it with the vector system mentioned above. At the time of the mathematician D'Alembert the question arose as to how two vectors should be added. The simple answer that was given was to use the parallelogram law. But some doubt remained as to the legitimacy of using this law to add two forces or two velocities. This doubt was resolved by the "argument" that vector addition must obey the following principles:

1. Vector addition must respect rotation. (If $T(\ \ )$ is a rotation operator and $\boldsymbol{a}$, $\boldsymbol{b}$ are vectors then $T(\boldsymbol{a} + \boldsymbol{b}) = T(\boldsymbol{a}) + T(\boldsymbol{b})$.)
2. Vector addition must operate as an Abelian group.
3. Vector addition must be continuous.
4. The addition of two vectors on the same line must involve simply putting one after the other along the line.

Using these principles, it can be proven that vector addition must obey the parallelogram law.

It is clear, however, that these principles are actually being used to construct the concept of the vector and the relations between vectors. This process was by no means arbitrary. Principles 1–4 could have been used to determine the addition of any two vectors, but the principles are not merely supported intuitions or assumptions about a well-defined area; they serve as constraints. Mathematicians obviously believe that it is impossible to work with vectors without using these principles, but the entire process was accomplished through imposing the constraints on a potential space of objects. We see that as the objects themselves are constructed, *constraints* and natural projections are turned into *axioms* about a space of objects.[3]

The mathematical objects that we add during expansions are viewed here as part of the genealogy of the concept of identity. They are created in the development of this concept, as it is reflected in the assignment of truth-values to new sentences. They do not exist "out there" like the continents, unless the continents themselves are created by expanding the concept of identity. Nevertheless, we cannot say that we invent these objects willfully or fancifully. Although there is an element of play in mathematics, it is not an empty play of symbols; rather, the words precede the objects they come to denote. Amusing questions such as "What is $3 - 9$?" and "What is a vector space with a non-integral number of dimensions?" pique our curiosity. They spur our thinking by offering an expression such that the assumption that there is an object that satisfies it violates some basic law, and we can often even prove logically that there is no object that could possibly be an answer to the question. But then we can construct an object that has precisely these properties.

This description serves to narrow the gap between Frege and the formalists. On the one hand, mathematical objects are not mere signs, and certainly not mere ink stains, as Frege claimed in his debate with the formalists, but accepting this does not make it necessary for us to see the signs as postdating the objects, as in the case of the continents. On the other hand, we can ask the formalists to restrict their use of metaphors such as calling mathematics a game and to avoid claiming that it is a free creation of the human mind. The criterion of inner consistency used by the formalists to limit mathematicians' freedom is not a sufficient restriction.[4] The way expansions force themselves on us, the way new objects are related to previous ones, and our interest in preserving the old laws as far as possible work together to form a solid foundation for constructing new mathematical objects such as the complex numbers.

---

[3] When a paradox is discovered we have a collapse of the space. See chapter 9 below.

[4] I do not intend to discuss all the formalists' claims, or Hilbert's claim that consistency is sufficient for truth in mathematics. I merely note that in order for this claim to be informative and not analytic there would have to be some distinction other than the identification of mathematical truth with consistency, but the formalists have not provided such a distinction.

I will now briefly discuss some questions and directions of thought suggested by the viewpoint presented here. The first question involves the validity of the laws of equality. Can we see them as arithmetical principles that we try to impose on objects rather than unquestionable axioms? Could we find ourselves giving up the transitivity principle for equality in the same way that we were forced to abandon the commutative law? Since the answer to this question depends on whether there are objects that require giving up basic principles in order to construct these objects, it cannot be determined in advance. This does not mean that the transitivity principle is not intuitive or fundamental, but rather that we may want to add objects whose description will require abandoning our familiar concept of equality. Although we could then describe the situation as a change in the concept of equality, this would not lessen the novelty involved. It would still be another stage in the concept of identity rather than something that is totally unconnected with this concept that requires abandoning the principle.

One particularly important suggestion that arises from our discussion is the possibility of expanding our theory about the identity of objects outside of mathematics. If this should turn out to be possible, it would be a proposal in the spirit of Kant, since it would claim that objects do not exist prior to the principles that apply to them, but are rather constituted by these principles. This suggestion implies that the judgment of identity does not provide us with truths about objects that are independent of our judgment of them, but rather we use such judgments to "consolidate" a multiplicity of words to create an object. When we "discovered" that the evening star was also the morning star we made use of the principle that "every heavenly body takes up one part of space" as a constraint on what we were willing to recognize as an object. This statement does not describe some knowledge about a general truth, but is rather a principle that we impose upon phenomena in order to construct objects that exist in space and time. After we construct an objective space of entities with relations that hold among them, it becomes a truth.

The principles have an a priori status not because we can know them irrespective of our experience, but because we impose them on our experience. However, there may be objects that can be constituted only by principles that contradict other respected principles. Yet this possibility, even though it contradicts the Kantian a priori (at least in one sense), is not a problem here. When, for example, we try to decide whether one elementary particle can be in two places at the same time, we base our decision not on some a priori principle but on some other constraint, such as the conservation of energy or the limiting speed of light. We abandon the attempt to impose our principles because something in the material that we are trying to force them on resists this imposition. But this metaphor only hints at the act of the construction of physical objects. The fact that the laws are violated is similar to what we do when we try to extend the power function while preserving the principle that all powers must always be greater than zero.

We may now return to our discussion of extensions prior to Frege's objections. We could perhaps read what I have said here into Leibniz's characterization of the products of extensions as creatures of the mind, hovering between being and nonbeing. Or perhaps we could say that the objects of mathematics are somewhere between actual continents and the realms of legend. But what we have achieved here is clear: the nominal description is developed and confirmed.

A negative multiplied by a negative equals a positive. But why?

The depiction offered here allows us to give better answers to basic questions in the algebra of negative numbers, as well as that of complex numbers. We all know that the multiplication of two negative numbers yields a positive number. The usual explanation given for this is through reference to the ring axioms.

The set of integers with "×" for multiplication and "+" for addition satisfies the ring axioms, and one can deduce from these axioms the property that $(-a)(-b) = ab$.
Indeed,

(1) $0 = a \times 0 = (-a) \times (b + (-b)) = (-a) \times b + (-a) \times (-b)$.
But
(2) $(-a) \times b = -(a \times b)$ is true since $0 = ((-a) + a) \times b = (-a) \times b + ab$ (and it can easily be deduced from the ring axioms that if $x + y = 0$ then $x = (-y)$ and $y = (-x)$).
Substituting (2) in (1) gives $-(a \times b) + (-a) \times (-b) = 0$. QED

But we may still ask if this is all that can be said about the law that the multiplication of negatives yields a positive. I would like to suggest an explanation that is mandated by the phenomenon of forced extensions, and present its advantages.

Let us begin with simple phenomena. Negative numbers are not given as a set where the ring axioms hold. Every negative number is the result of a subtraction operation that cannot be made between positive numbers. We add the subtraction operation to our language, which includes the ring operations, and we may then consider some impossible subtractions, such as the expression "$1 - 4$". There are many other such expressions that cannot be actualized within the set of positive numbers.

However, the impossibility of this actualization is not absolute, and in fact depends on the laws we are interested in preserving. Pascal was certain that the result of such expressions is actually zero. I do not believe that this is complete nonsense, as a junior high school teacher might reply to a student who said that. We can argue as follows: taking 4 from 1 cannot result in a number greater than zero, and the only number that is not greater than zero is zero itself. We do have, then, a certain consideration that would lead to a position like that of Pascal. But this consideration does not bar other possible developments. We have the experience to know that one non-arbitrary expansion does not bar another non-arbitrary expansion.

We might propose rejecting Pascal's principles, and constructing new objects according to other principles, as indeed occurred in the development of mathematics. In general, this might be described as the attempt to mold the behavior of these "impossible" expressions according to the knowledge we have. In other words, we analyze the positive number system and the laws that govern it, and consider their effect on these expressions – that is, we take laws that are valid for positive numbers and ask what they force this expression to be. For example, we can show that the law

$$a - (b - c) = a - b + c,$$

which is valid in the case of positive numbers, forces us to identify the expression

$$\text{"}3 - (1 - 4)\text{"}$$

with "6."

Moreover, we must identify

$$\text{"}3 + (1 - 4)\text{"}$$

with "0" if we want to preserve the law

$$a + (b - c) = (a - c) + b.$$

Likewise, if we wish to preserve certain laws, we have to identify "$1 - 4$" with "$2 - 5$" as well as with "$0 - 3$," and so on. We can thus obtain a class of sentences of this form: if we preserve the laws in the set S, then the identities in the set T must be judged as true.[5] Given the proper S which holds for positive numbers, e.g., the axioms of a ring, we will see why the multiplication of negative numbers must be positive.

According to this explanation, negative integers and the laws that apply to them are taken directly from non-negative integers (i.e., the natural numbers) and the laws that apply to them. The point is that we do not assume a priori that the ring axioms hold for negative integers, and use this assumption to prove our arguments. On the contrary, we have a genealogy of the integers, and the laws that hold in that domain. Among other things, we can account for the origin of the ring axioms. Moreover, it is now clear that there are certain degrees of freedom in developing the domain of positive rational numbers into the domain of all rational numbers, which is usually obscured by the algebraic explanation.

I believe that is what underlies Peacock's principle of equivalence of permanent forms, as described in the first chapter of this book. The laws that hold in a mathematical field are not arbitrary axioms, but a natural continuation of the laws that hold for positive integers.

Now we are in a position to answer the question posed to Peacock's principle by Hamilton's quaternions. Commutativity is a law which we naturally want to maintain, but it turns out that this is not always possible. Still, it is unnecessary to retain all the laws that are true for the original model. We can only retain some of the laws, and we can arrive at a different expansion of the model each time we try, depending on which laws we decide to keep.

This is a problem for Robinson's concept of model completeness, which requires that all the generalizations of the original model should be kept. In fact, it is actually possible to develop a different structure that retains different laws – for example, one in which the multiplication of negative numbers is not always positive. This should be no surprise in light of the possibility of forced expansions that are not strongly forced. In fact, from any given structure we can develop a whole tree of structures, rather than merely a monotonic sequence.

We can understand the laws of complex numbers in the same way. We take certain laws that hold for real numbers, and force these laws onto the complex field. It turns out to be impossible to extend the linear order of the real numbers to the complex field at the same time as we retain certain other properties. But it would be conceivable to expand

---

[5] I hope there is no need for elaborate technical definitions here, and that the reader understands this. What I would like to do here is to show the advantages of this viewpoint.

the order laws while other laws are given up, which would provide us with a different expansion of the real numbers.

So far we have been discussing external expansions without even mentioning the question of the basis from which such expansions are performed, if such a basis indeed exists. Here we encounter a classical view with many variations, the most famous of which was offered by Kronecker in his remark, "The natural numbers were created by God; all else is the work of man." In this section I suggest that it is not necessary to adopt this view, and I offer a detailed sketch of how we can avoid the first part of Kronecker's remark.

Before embarking on this let me just note that the second part of Kronecker's remark is not without its problems either. It might be argued that the possibility of reducing the complex numbers to ordered pairs of real numbers, or the fact that they can be obtained from other objects, does not prove that the complex numbers do not really exist. For example, the astonishing applicability of the complex numbers and their deep connection with the real numbers, which lets us use the former to explain properties of the latter, can be a basis for arguing that the complex numbers actually do exist, if we add a few assumptions.

But even if we agree that the fact that something was created by an external extension does not prevent it from existing, we remain with the question of which numbers could serve as the primitive base and which are the result of external expansions. We are interested in finding out the absolute minimum of numbers that must be used as a starting point from which all other mathematical objects can be constructed. The fact that we must begin with something may seem unavoidable. Even if we consider the larger numbers and the relations between them as the result of an expansion, which, as I said in chapter 1, may perhaps have been hinted at by Wittgenstein, we must still assume some basic mathematical objects and some functions defined on them.

But there is an even more elegant starting point. I will present a primary set of sentences which I shall interpret as sentences about ordinals from which we can begin without any assumptions whatsoever. This set could be developed from a model that does not assume any natural numbers at all. I will thus be presenting a criticism of Kronecker's view from the other direction – if human beings created the complex numbers, then they created all the numbers.

The claim I present here is that the ordinals and the relations between them can be described as an expansion of the predicate calculus. This expansion is required in order properly to formulate the EI law. Let me start with an explanation of the EI law.

The inference law EI allows us to move from a sentence of the form:

(1) $\exists v\, S(v)$,

in which "v" is a schematic sign for variables such as x, y, z, to a sentence of the form:

(2) $S(a)$,

in which a must be a *new* name in the derivation. Violating this last limitation is an illegitimate move. For example, if the sentence

(3) Pitzi is walking slowly

precedes the sentence

(4) There is at least one ant in the world

in the derivation, we are not allowed to use the name 'Pitzi' to denote one of the ants whose existence is posited in sentence (4). This is because we are not entitled to deduce from (3) and (4) alone that Pitzi is an ant. We must therefore say that *all* we know of the new name in (2) is that it designates an ant.

Having made this qualification, we may ask how to *justify* introducing a new name. One explanation naturally suggests itself: sentence (4) entails the existence of at least one ant, and so we can choose that ant and call it by a new name. However, being alert to the problem of "choice" in set theory, we may want to rephrase this explanation. We should claim that the reason we can derive (2) from (1) is that it is possible to call someone or something by a name and get a sentence of the form "$S(a)$".[6]

But this explanation is still problematic because what it allows us to do is move from (1) to:

(5) It is possible to call one of the S's by a name,

rather than (2). Sentence (5) is not the same as (2) and the move from (1) to (5), although perhaps justified, invokes a modal operator, while no logician would admit that first-order logic requires modal completions.

But we can easily show that a in (2) cannot be a name. It is impossible to deduce a sentence such as

(6) Johnny is an ant

from (4), even if we make sure that "Johnny" is a new name in the

---

[6] Lemmon (1961) contains a detailed examination of this point.

derivation. Every sentence of the form "*a* is an ant" says more than (4). Indeed, it is easy to construct a model in which (4) is true and (6) is false.

Here is another way of showing that the "intuitiveness" of EI is misleading. Consider the following sentence:

(7) Bambi is a nameless dog.

It seems that this sentence cannot be true. If it were true then "Bambi" would be Bambi's name, and we would have to conclude that Bambi does have a name. On the other hand, the sentence:

(8) There is a nameless dog

is a true sentence, since we all know that dogs without names exist in the world. Thus, if we allow EI, it will be possible to derive the false sentence (7) from the true sentence (8).

There are several ways of dealing with this problem, two of which I will discuss. Fine (1985) requires a new category of objects, so that alongside concrete ants and horses there are non-concrete ants and horses that are needed for an elegant account of the universal generalization (UG) and EI laws.[7] Gupta (1968) handles the problem by expanding the category of signs rather than the category of objects. The expression "a" in the formula "$S(a)$" does not designate an object; it only has the syntactic form of a name. Similarly, the sentence "$S(a)$" is not a real sentence but an imaginary one. We add new signs that imitate names and sentences in order to facilitate logical derivations. What we gain from this is the ability to replace a quantified sentence with a simpler one (and unsurprisingly this is somewhat awkward). All we need to show – and this Gupta does – is that this is a conservative expansion of first-order logic.

I will now informally explain Gupta's treatment of EI so as to clarify its relation to ordinal numbers (and definite descriptions). Suppose we have a particular system of axioms in a first-order language. In order to perform the transition required by EI, we have to add new signs for every existential sentence. Thus, for each sentence of the form "$\exists v\, S(v)$" we will have to add a special new imaginary name a and a new imaginary sentence "$S(a)$."

To allow for complicated proofs, we have to consider iterative applications of EI, as well as UI, UG, EG, and perhaps other laws. I call this process "the preparation of a system." Let me start with an example.

---

[7] The UG law suffers from an analogous problem to that of EI, involving the impossibility of deriving $\forall x\, S(x)$ from $S(a)$.

Suppose we have a system consisting of the following three sentences:

(S1) $\exists x \, S(x)$.
(S2) $\exists x \, P(x)$.
(S3) $\forall x (S(x) \rightarrow P(x))$.

The preparation of this system results in an ordered pair $\langle A, B \rangle$ of sets – a set of imaginary names A and a set of imaginary sentences B, which are closed under the application of the EI and UI. This entails that $A \supseteq \{a, b\}^8$ and $B \supseteq \{S(a), P(b), S(a) \rightarrow P(a), S(b) \rightarrow P(b)\}$.

For any given set of axioms D, here is an informal description of the algorithm that yields the corresponding preparation $\langle A_{\mathrm{D}}, B_{\mathrm{D}} \rangle$. Put the sentences in D in prenex normal form.[9] Add a new imaginary name for every sentence of the form $\exists v S(v)$. In case there are no existential sentences, substitute a new name for the first general sentence. Next, substitute these new signs in the corresponding open sentences $S(v)$. Every new imaginary name that was added must now be substituted in every general sentence of our system. Having done this, we construct the ordered pair $\langle A_{\mathrm{D}}{}^1, B_{\mathrm{D}}{}^1 \rangle$. It contains a set of all the new imaginary names we introduced, and a set of all the imaginary sentences obtained by substituting the names contained in the first set in the corresponding open and general sentences. If the set $B_{\mathrm{D}}{}^1$ contains new existential sentences (as a result of substitution in general sentences), we reapply the same process to this system to obtain $\langle A_{\mathrm{D}}{}^2, B_{\mathrm{D}}{}^2 \rangle$, $\langle A_{\mathrm{D}}{}^3, B_{\mathrm{D}}{}^3 \rangle$ and so on. Having this sequence, we define $\langle A_{\mathrm{D}}, B_{\mathrm{D}} \rangle = \lim_{n \to \infty} \langle A_{\mathrm{D}}{}^n, B_{\mathrm{D}}{}^n \rangle$. We know that the system of imaginary names A and sentences B that are required to allow for an application of the EI law satisfies

$$A \supseteq A_{\mathrm{D}}, \qquad B \supseteq B_{\mathrm{D}}.$$

Now, what happens in a case where we know that only one object satisfies $S(x)$? In such a case we can introduce a new name that really names the object. This is a familiar move in mathematics. Yet it is not an imaginary name that we introduce into our derivation by EI. One way to express the difference is to note that this second kind of move requires naming, an act done at the meta-level which is not a step in the deduction, while the "name" guaranteed by EI *is* part of the proof. There is another difference: the naming can be done only if $\exists ! x S(x)$ is

---

[8] Mere inclusion suffices for my purposes.
[9] A sentence in prenex normal form is one in which all quantifiers come at the left and govern the whole sentence. For every sentence, there is a logically equivalent sentence in prenex normal form.

true and known to be true, while adding an imaginary name does not require it to be true at all.

If we have a sentence of the form "$\exists x(P(x) \land \forall y(P(y) \rightarrow y = x) \land Q(x))$" (i.e., "The P is Q") as an axiom, we can even improve on the EI law and suggest the following law: a sentence of the form

(9) $\exists x(P(x) \land \forall y(P(y) \rightarrow y = x \land Q(x)))$

implies

(10) $Q(\textit{the } P)$,

"*the P*" being a new imaginary name. This method of constructing imaginary names ensures that they have no meaning outside the context of the sentence from which they originate. This is in harmony with Russell's theory. Although Russell's analysis of sentences in natural language of the form "The P is Q" tells us that we must view them as (9) "exactly one P is Q," we can, if we wish to preserve the formal similarity, identify them with the logical equivalent "$Q(\textit{the } P)$." In other words, the expression "the P" is an imaginary name we get in preparing a system including (9) for the derivation of (10). The corresponding imaginary sentence is "$Q(\textit{the } P)$."[10]

To get the numerals for ordinal numbers we have to look at the axioms of order:

(R1) $\exists x! \, \forall y(y \neq x \rightarrow R(x, y))$
(R2) $\forall x \, \exists y \, \forall z(R(x, y) \land (R(x, z) \land z \neq y \rightarrow R(y, z)))$
(R3) $\forall x \forall y \forall z(R(x, y) \land R(y, z) \rightarrow R(x, z))$
(R4) $\forall x \neg R(x, x)$
(R5) $\forall x \forall y(R(x, y) \lor R(y, x))$.

In preparing this system we start by introducing a new imaginary name a in the first axiom. We then have to substitute a in R2–R4. We get a set of imaginary sentences which includes an existential sentence that results from the substitution of a in R2. This sentence yields a new imaginary name b. Substituting b in the original R2 we get another new imaginary existential yielding a new name c, and so on. To construct the set B_R we substitute all the imaginary names in R2–R5 as well as in

(R1') $\forall y(y \neq a \rightarrow R(a, y))$.

---

[10] To the best of my knowledge, Russell never saw his analysis of expressions of the form "The P is Q" in the general way introduced here. It was enough for him to say that there are good reasons (logical and epistemological) for the claim that expresssions such as "the P" are not real names (as claimed by Frege), and that the best way to analyze them is by viewing them as quantified sentences in disguise.

Every time we add a new imaginary name we get a better approximation of $\langle A_R\, B_R \rangle$. If we close this system to deduction we get a uniquely determined set of sentences which includes sentences such as "$R(a,\, b)$," "$R(a,\, c)$," "$R(b,\, c)$," "$\sim R(b,\, a)$," etc. I can now state my thesis: the ordinals "the first," "the second," "the third," ... are the imaginary names $a,\, b,\, c,\, \ldots$ in the set A_R. Moreover, what is true of ordinals is given by the set of imaginary sentences B_R.[11]

This view is very similar to that of Benacerraf (1965) who wrote:

To be the number 3 is no more and no less than to be preceded by 2, 1 and possibly 0 and to be followed by 4, 5, ... *Any* object can *play the role* of 3; that is, any object can be the third element in some progression. What is peculiar to 3 is that it defines this role. It does so not by being a paradigm of any object that plays it, but by representing the relation that any third member of a progression bears to the rest of the progression (p. 291).

Compare the claim that "If *a* is a name of an ant, we cannot assume more about *a* save that it is an ant" (when we move from $\exists v\, A(v)$ to $A(a)$ by EI) with "It must be possible to individuate those objects independently of the role they play in the structure. But this is exactly what cannot be done with numbers" (ibid.). The only difference I can see is that Benacerraf is speaking about "structures" and not ants, but this is accounted for in our analysis by replacing "structure" with a schematic relation that satisfies the axioms of order. The account proposed above, if it is valid, may be viewed as an explication of Benacerraf's insight which does not invoke problematic notions such as *abstract structure, role,* or *systems of relations in intension,* or talk about *the set of all progressions.*[12]

By now it should be clear that I am *not* claiming that the system *R* is an implicit definition of ordinals. The ordinals are not the set of objects that satisfy the system R1–R5 and its extension. The relation "$R(\quad,\quad)$" is taken as a schema; after specifying "$R(\quad,\quad)$" *a* becomes a name such as "the first day" or "the first person to reach the moon," depending on the content of the relation that we substitute for "$R(\quad,\quad)$". Substituting a specific relation for "$R(\quad,\quad)$" results in a set of true sentences, and only then do the quantifiers range over a set of objects. When "$R(\quad,\quad)$"

---

[11] In the discussion above I assumed that sets exist, or else I could not have defined the set $\langle A_D,\, B_D \rangle = \lim_{n \to \infty} \langle A_D{}^n,\, B_D{}^n \rangle$.

[12] I am not claiming that ordinal numbers are not objects, since there is a method proposed by Fine for solving the problem of the EI law that requires the addition of a special category of objects (arbitrary objects) rather than imaginary names. But this is consistent with Benacerraf's recent qualification (1998) of his earlier argument (1983) Similarly, I am not claiming that there are no structures, but only that in order to explain Benacerraf's insight we do not need to appeal to structures.

is schematic, a and b are "the first" and "the second," without any qualification.

Ordinals are necessary because they allow us to eliminate quantifiers in a specific set of axioms. The EI law enables us to read a quantified sentence as if it were a simpler one. We must compensate for this, however, by adding a new category of signs. Natural language does the same by using devices such as definite descriptions and pronouns. We count "the first," "the second," etc., thus preparing ourselves to understand relations that Nature and our everyday experience present. It is in the context of this general method that we must understand ordinals, and not by viewing them as mere names for sets or for objects of a different kind.

Nevertheless, at a later stage we can view imaginary sentences such as "$R(a, b)$" as if they were true sentences, and expand the machinery of quantification over them. We would then claim that there is an ordinal between a and c, treating them as if they were true names. This should not be new to the reader, since a completely analogous reification occurred in the case of the negative and the complex numbers.

The position proposed here has an important metaphysical advantage in that it does not distinguish between kinds of mathematical objects and other existing things. Some numbers are more primary than others – the natural numbers, for instance, precede the negative numbers, because the former can be obtained from a simpler basis – but this primacy does not make them different kinds of objects. The picture presented here is thus not a Fregean one. What enabled us to avoid Frege's dreaded psychologism is the recognition that we have a rational procedure here. The view that expansions can be subject to logic allows us to accept formalism without endangering the objectivity of mathematics. At the same time it does not reduce mathematics to an interesting but empty game or mere words. But this is not the last word on the relation between forced expansions and realism.

Gödel's argument

The concept of forced expansion has been sufficiently articulated by now so as to facilitate finding such expansions in other settings. In the present chapter I will examine one of Gödel's arguments, which has not yet been given the attention it deserves, but which is easy to disclose once we are aware of non-arbitrary developments of concepts (I shall call it "Gödel's second argument"). If we reformulate this argument in the terminology that has been developed here, we can understand Gödel as claiming that the very existence of forced expansions proves (a) the existence of concepts and at the same time (b) naturally leads to the possibility of perceiving them. In the first part of the present chapter I set forth Gödel's argument in broad outline.

In the second part I examine the notion of the perception of concepts as it arises from Gödel's descriptions. Here I try to show how this argument is relevant to the lively discussion about this notion of Gödel's, which has developed around Gödel's more famous argument deriving our intuition of objects from the fact that the axioms of set theory are forced on us (call this "Gödel's first argument"). Familiarity with the phenomenon of expansions allows us to refine Gödel's picture and make his views seem more plausible.

In the third part of the chapter I discuss Gödel's argument in favor of realism for concepts. It seems that this argument needs to be amended, since it does not take seriously the phenomenon of expansions that are not strongly forced. After suggesting such an amendment, I investigate one way in which Gödel could have made his argument valid.

A PRELIMINARY PRESENTATION

Using a collection of Gödel's remarks edited by Wang Hao, one can clearly see Gödel's argument for the existence of concepts, which is relevant to our purposes here: "If there is nothing sharp to begin with, it is hard to understand how, in many cases, a vague concept can uniquely determine a sharp one without even the *slightest* freedom of choice" (quoted from Wang 1996, p. 233).

What immediately captures our attention is the phrase "without even the *slightest* freedom of choice." I believe it is possible to read this argument in the terminology of forced expansions, but in order to do this I must first present one reservation, which is due to the fact that Gödel was discussing a wider variety of transitions from one concept to another.

Indeed, it is easy to recognize that Gödel had in mind not only forced expansions but also the transition from a vague concept to a sharp and clear one. Here is an example:

> If we begin with a vague intuitive concept, how can we find a sharp concept to correspond to it faithfully? The answer is that the sharp concept is there all along, only we did not perceive it clearly at first. This is similar to our perception of an animal first far away and then nearby. We had not perceived the sharp concept of mechanical procedures before Turing, who brought us to the right perspective (quoted from Wang 1996, p. 232).

Turing's definition of computability is a sort of conceptual analysis, and does not seem similar to a forced expansion. It is nevertheless clear that *some* of Gödel's examples of forced transitions from one concept to another belong to the category we are interested in. When Gödel characterizes the transitions he is discussing, he describes a process very similar to the one analyzed in the preceding chapters of the present book:

> The precise concept meant by the intuitive idea of velocity clearly is $\mathrm{d}s/\mathrm{d}t$ and the precise concept meant by "size" (as opposed to "shape"), e.g. of a lot, clearly is equivalent to Peano measure in the case where either concept is applicable. In these cases the solutions are *unquestionably* unique, which here is due to the fact that only they satisfy certain axioms which, on closer inspection, we find to be undeniably implied in the concept we had. For example, congruent figures have the same area, a part has no larger size than the whole, etc. (Wang 1996, p. 233).

And yet, even though this argument is not a matter of secondary importance, Gödel did not take the trouble to elaborate it or even formulate it carefully. Gödel does not distinguish between vague and intuitive concepts. In some places he speaks of the transition from vague to sharp concepts, while in others the transition is from intuitive to sharp concepts, and in yet other places he uses both terms together.

But vagueness is not the same as intuitiveness. Moreover, the examples he brings demonstrate that he did not have a clear notion of vagueness. As mentioned, before Cantor's definition the concept of number was vague in the sense that there was a whole space of sets on which it was not defined, but its boundaries were clear in that it applied to all finite sets and no infinite sets. In contrast, the concept of computability is more of an unclear concept than a vague one. Another example of Gödel's is the concept of velocity. This concept was not vague before it was redefined by means of the derivative in any sense that I can think of.

I must therefore state my reservations about Gödel's argument before I undertake an analysis of it. Gödel speaks about different transitions from one concept to another, which he considers to be forced. The examples he brings and the way he performs the procedure suggest that he wanted to include as many cases as possible in his description. However, only some of these cases belong to the realm of expansions. My discussion will focus on forced expansions, but it will not be limited to examples of this sort.

Now for the argument itself. The uniqueness of Gödel's view stands out against the background of the discussion in the previous chapters. There we saw that the phenomenon of expansions generally leads us in non-realist directions. Consider, for example, Kronecker's position, which was analyzed in chapter 6. It is useful to compare Gödel's argument with Gauss's position that, since concepts are the creations of our mind, we can define them in any way that is convenient. Gödel turns this around: he argues that the fact that we do *not* simply define concepts in ways that are convenient, but that expansions are actually forced upon us uniquely, proves that they are not merely the products of our mind.

Gödel's argument in favor of realism makes use of mathematical *concepts*, not merely mathematical objects. Gödel ascribes a reality to concepts which goes beyond the semantic role that we ascribe to them in order to analyze sentences in an extensional way.[1] The reality of concepts is for Gödel independent of the role of predicates in sentences; we can grasp concepts in a sense which is closely related to the ability to perceive empirical objects.[2]

---

[1] In this I follow Dummett's distinction (1973, pp. 190–2).

[2] Perhaps this is also what enabled Gödel to see the existence of paradoxes as an argument for the existence of concepts, while Frege saw them as undermining the entire notion of concepts (see chapter 9 below).

QUASI-PERCEPTION OR PERCEPTION

As we have seen, Gödel based both of his propositions – that concepts exist, and that they are perceived – on his claim that the transition from one concept to another is forced and unique. Conclusions very close to these also appear in Gödel's famous argument, which is still a lively issue in the philosophy of mathematics: "But despite their remoteness from sense experience, we do have something like a perception of the objects of set theory, as is seen from the fact that the axioms force themselves upon us as being true" (Gödel 1983, pp. 483-4).

Here too Gödel claims that "the axioms force themselves upon us." We can thus ask whether the discussion in the previous section can shed light on the nature of this forcing or on any possible conceptual connection between it and the notion of perception that is based on it. In the present section I will leave the problem of the reality of concepts on one side and will focus on the question of whether they are perceived. I will return to the issue of realism in the next section.

We must proceed carefully, since we are trying to preserve the multifaceted nature of Gödel's view while developing it in the direction suggested by Gödel's remarks. For this purpose I have chosen to develop Gödel's view in two stages. The first is a weaker one that is committed only to the analogy with perception, while the second contains a program for analyzing the concept of perception or intuition. These two stages are two possible interpretations of Gödel, neither of which is clearly favored by the text. I will begin with the weaker stage, which is included in the stronger one.

The weak position relies on the idea that some development is forced on us. It creates non-trivial analogies between the perception of objects and the perception of concepts. These analogies are sufficient to show that the perception of concepts is not the same as the perception of physical objects, but only something similar. Here are some of these analogies, collected from various places in Gödel's writings.

1. We can sharpen our view of a particular object by coming closer to it. Analogously, we can sharpen our grasp of a particular concept by going from a partially defined concept to a sharper one. This can be elucidated as follows. When a concept is not defined everywhere we cannot distinguish between objects for which it is not defined. Before we expanded the concept of number we could not distinguish between denumerable and nondenumerable infinities – there was just "infinity." Only after we have performed the expansion can we distinguish different

varieties of infinity. In the same way, what we have before an expansion is a vague perception of something, as if we are looking at it from afar. When we get nearer our perception becomes clearer and we can distinguish more details of the thing.

The uniqueness of the expansion of the concept of number is important here, because we are supposed to be coming closer to the concept through the piecemeal expansions of something similar to what we have called stages of concepts, and one cannot come closer in two different ways that result in seeing two different pictures. If this were possible, we could not say there was something we were coming closer to.[3]

2. Two things that we see from afar may look alike, but when we come closer to them we see that they are actually different. Gödel brings the example of the concepts of continuity and smoothness, and we can add the example of the concepts of cardinal and ordinal numbers. Although we can see a difference between the latter pair of concepts even without the expansion of the concept of number to infinite sets, this difference does not seem very significant, and we can pass from one to the other quite easily. But after the development of the concept of ordinal numbers in the theory of sets it became clear that this is a separate concept.[4] Two infinite sets can have the same cardinal number without having the same ordinal number. Only after the expansion of these concepts beyond finite sets can we see that the arithmetic of the ordinal numbers is completely different from that of the cardinal numbers.[5]

3. Illusions can occur in the perception of concepts just as in the perception of objects. Here we have a Kantian tradition connecting the illusions brought about by our intellect with those brought about by sensory perception. Gödel follows this tradition in his explanation of the source of paradoxes (see chapter 9).

4. Things can be seen from different aspects. This is certainly true of visually perceived objects, and Gödel believed that it is true in the case of

---

3 Gibson's (1950) theory of perception emphasizes the conceptual connection between vision and movement. Gibson arrived at this notion because he believes that vision is the interaction of a living creature that moves and changes its place within its environment. This is a primary concept for him, while a single "snapshot" without motion is derivative from it. From this viewpoint, Gödel emphasized a central aspect of vision.

4 The definition of the cardinal numbers that makes use of the ordinal numbers is far from showing that the same concept is involved. It would be artificial to claim that this definition is a philosophical explication of the concept of cardinality. It would be better to see it as an attempt to nest the cardinal numbers within the ordinal numbers.

5 Gödel brings these examples in order to explain certain unintuitive results, such as the possibility of covering a square with a continuous line. This stems from the fact that we confuse two or more concepts with one another because we do not have an analysis of them.

the perception of concepts as well. Thanks to Turing, Gödel claims, we have achieved the correct perspective on the concept of computability. We can, so to speak, walk around the concept and see its various projections. In order to understand this quality of the perception of concepts, we do not need an extensional view of them, in which concepts that have the same extension are identical. Gödel would apparently have taken a stronger view, in which the identity of the extensions would be necessary or provable. Thus we can grasp a concept under a particular definition and then under an equivalent one, after which we may come to see that they are identical. This is analogous to the possibility of perceiving the same object from different perspectives.

5. Gödel was aware that we do not perceive a concept all at once, but only with great effort. He nevertheless retains the analogy by claiming that perception is not immediate. This shows us how seriously Gödel took the analogy, as wherever it seemed to fail he quickly amended it to show that the failure is only apparent.

6. When your eyes are open you have no choice but to see what you see, and by the same token when you think about certain axioms you have no choice about whether or not to accept them: you cannot deny them.

The weaker interpretation of Gödel's claim is contained in these analogies and, possibly, similar ones. The strong interpretation is that the perception of concepts is actual perception, not merely analogous to perception. To make this claim we have to see the perception of sticks and stones and the perception of concepts as two different subtypes of some more general type of perception.[6]

This stronger interpretation of Gödel's claim is similar to an important aspect of Kant's notion of intuition, as elucidated by Hintikka. Hintikka (1969) remarks that Kantian intuition is not tied to sensory perception by definition, as can be seen by the very expression "intellectual intuition" used to denote one type of intuition. He claims that an intuition is a singular representation that refers to one particular thing. Although Kant insists that human beings cannot have any other kind of intuition but the sensory one, this does not involve the essence of intuition but is rather

---

[6] In this way we do not have to commit ourselves to Maddy's (1990) interpretation of perception, in which we see sets with our physical eyes, although we are no longer speaking about something that is merely similar to sensory perception. Maddy rejects the idea, presented here, that there are two different types of perception, claiming that there is only one type. She also avoids speaking about the perception of concepts, limiting her discussion to the perception of sets. This I believe is a result of not giving any place to what I have called the second argument.

a limitation of the human mind.[7] Unlike Kant, however, Gödel did not tell us what the different kinds of perception have in common, and, as we shall see, he was not using Kant's notion of intuition.

If we want to make use of the strong interpretation of Gödel, we must connect the analogies he suggested to a definition of this sort. These analogies provide a means for beginning to analyze the concept of perception. They should be seen as general properties of a more abstract notion of perception, and we hope to find a single concept from which all these analogies are derived.

We can indeed find such an abstract concept of intuition in Gödel's writings. For example, he says, "Understanding a primitive concept is by an abstract intuition" (Wang 1996, p. 217). This can be seen even more clearly in his dissatisfaction with Kant's concept of intuition: "Our real intuition is finite, and in fact, limited to something small. Kantian intuition is too weak a concept of idealization of our intuition. I prefer a strong concept of idealization of it" (Wang 1996, p. 217).[8]

We must therefore look for a concept of intuition that is stronger than Kant's. Our present concept of perception should be viewed as a paradigm case of a more general notion of perception. From this viewpoint the situation seems similar to what happened to the concept of computability. Gödel could have claimed that it is possible to analyze the concept of perception in a way that is generally similar to the way the concept of computability was analyzed. In that case too computation with pencil and paper is probably primary, but at the end of the analysis we achieve an abstract, unambiguous concept.[9]

Gödel believed that the entire issue of intuition was being discussed on a very low level, like the atomic theory at the time of Democritus. He apparently thought that his analogies were a step in the direction of a clearer definition of the concept of intuition. They thus resembled constraints that we preserve when we expand a function. We do not have a definition of integrals in which we see that all sorts of functions are integrable; rather, we have some laws which we extract from our intuitions in this area, such as the law that an area which includes another

---

[7] Something similar can be found in the view that empirical and a priori intuition are two types of one concept of intuition.

[8] The word "idealization" here is used technically by Gödel to refer to the generalization and abstraction of a system from something that is given intuitively.

[9] It would be interesting to see if Gödel's disagreement with the claim that the mind is a Turing machine is connected with this ability of the mind to grasp concepts. As far as I know, Gödel never said anything about the connection between these two views of his.

area cannot be smaller than the area it includes. In this reading, Gödel's analogies are like laws guiding the analysis of the concept of intuition.

We can only guess how these analogies are supposed to contribute to forming such a definition. We study sensory perception and extract some of its general qualities, and then we propose analogous conceptual qualities. Thus the idea of sharpening a picture, and the idea of an aspect of the object can all be generalized and perhaps even formalized. We can speak of a possible picture of a state of affairs, and assume the existence of an order relation between different pictures of the same state of affairs, in which one picture is considered sharper than another if details that are not distinguishable in the first picture are distinguishable in the second one.[10] The transition from a less sharp picture to a sharper one amounts to approaching the perceived object. All these qualities will be defined in a general way that is not restricted to sensory perception. According to the stronger interpretation of Gödel, we must see him as hoping that in time it would be possible to expand the concept of perception, so that his analogies were intended to further this goal.[11]

A COMPARISON OF GÖDEL'S TWO ARGUMENTS

This interpretation of Gödel offers an apparently more reasonable view of his ideas, which have generally not been accepted by contemporary philosophers. Parsons developed the notion of the perception of concepts in order to present an improved reconstruction of Gödel's argument. In an early paper he writes: "Here [in the first argument] he seems to conclude from the evident character of certain statements which we might express as 'intuitions that,' to the existence of 'intuitions of.' The premise may be disputed, but even if it is granted the inference seems to be a non sequitur" (Parsons, 1979–80, p. 146).

In a later paper, however, Parsons (1995, p. 65) ascribes a more important role to the perception of concepts, considering it a natural way of preserving Gödel's first argument. Here Parsons is assuming that Gödel

---

[10] It would be interesting, for example, to see whether the expressions of the type "$F(T, A)$" could be used for generalizing the concept of getting closer to something.

[11] It is also possible to claim that there is no real difference between the two ways of interpreting Gödel. But then the question arises as to what could be the basis for such a position. One possible basis is Wittgenstein's notion of family resemblance. We have a concept of perception, and we use it in all sorts of ways, but there is no one thing that all of these uses have in common. This would justify seeing no difference between two concepts with a multiplicity of analogies between them, on the one hand, and a single concept, on the other. This view of concepts would, however, have been rejected by Gödel, partly because of his non-nominalist view on concepts, which is grounded in the phenomenon of forced transition from a vague concept to a sharp one.

believed concepts to be the components of propositions, and thought that the perception of a proposition implies the perceptions of the concepts involved in it as well.[12]

But even someone who believes that there is something more than sentences, recognizing the existence of concepts as well, does not have to accept the claim that a proposition is composed of concepts. The best example of this is Frege, who considered concepts to be part of the world, rather than the components of thoughts. Moreover, it is not clear why the perception of a proposition should imply the perception of the concepts of which it is composed. After all, we can imagine a situation in which we perceive complex things without perceiving their components (for example, at a certain distance we can see that there is a written text even though we cannot read the words constituting this text).

What I am interested in here, however, is not Gödel's first argument in and of itself, but rather the fact that Parsons understands Gödel's notion of the perception of concepts in light of that argument. Here is how he puts it:

"The objects of set theory" for him [Gödel] include *concepts*, and rational evidence of a proposition goes with clear perception of the concepts in it. My own tendency is to distinguish sharply between the understanding of a predicate and apprehension of any objects associated with them; for it to be evident to me that every natural number has a successor is no doubt an exercise of the concept of number, but I would not characterize it as apprehension or "perception" of that concept; it can be just evident to someone who is skeptical about the whole idea of concepts (Parsons 1998).

Parsons rejects the attempt to deduce that concepts are perceived from the fact that the principles which use these concepts are evidently true. This would lead us to believe that Gödel's transition from the fact that the axioms are forced on us to the perception of concepts is a transition from the evident truth of the axioms of set theory to the perception of Platonic objects. It thus seems that Parsons is discussing Gödel's argument for *concepts* being perceived in light of Gödel's first argument – the argument that *sets* are perceived or quasi-perceived. But it is not obvious that the two are identical. Even the claim that the objects of set theory include concepts is not evident, partly because Gödel stated that the perception of concepts is different from the perception of objects, and partly because he distinguished between set theory and the theory of concepts. Thus not

---

[12] Parsons' words are "This, I think, is the unstated premiss of an inference that at first sight appears to be a *non sequitur*" (ibid.).

only does the first argument fail to be a complete statement of Gödel's views, but it is not even clear that Gödel would have relied on it as an argument in favor of the existence of concepts or the possibility of perceiving or even quasi-perceiving concepts.

If we do not follow Parsons' lead, but instead analyze the perception of concepts according to the idea that concepts are forced on us, as I have presented it here, then Gödel's position seems more coherent. This enables us to respond to the conclusion of Parsons' remarks in the quotation just presented. Gödel claimed that the fact that concepts force themselves on us allows us to deduce that they must exist. Therefore, Parsons' conclusion that anyone who does not accept the existence of concepts can avoid Gödel's argument does not do justice to Gödel's view. For Gödel at least thought that his argument could compel his opponents to acknowledge the existence of concepts; he did not assume that they exist so that he could present his argument, as Parsons' criticism implies.

If we decide to interpret Gödel's notion of the perception of concepts in the weak way we described above, then Parsons' criticism must take into account the fact that Gödel provides a set of non-trivial analogies. Parsons interprets the claim that concepts are forced on us as if it means that the propositions that contain them are evidently true, thus weakening the basis of Gödel's argument; at the same time he interprets the idea of perception literally, thus strengthening the conclusion of the argument.

I will end this section with an examination of the possibility of reading the first argument in terms of the second one. In other words, we should try to understand the idea that axioms force themselves on us, which appears in the first argument, in light of the notion that concepts force themselves on us, which appears in the second one. One indication of how we can do this can be found in Gödel's introduction to his essay on Cantor, in which he develops his first argument. This introduction contains an entire page in which Gödel claims that the concept of number is forced on us, and that there is only one way of expanding it. The following is part of that page:

This question, of course, could arise only after the concept of "number" has been extended to infinite sets; hence it might be doubted if this extension can be effected in a uniquely determined manner . . . Closer examination, however, shows that Cantor's definition of infinite numbers really has this character of uniqueness (Gödel 1983a, p. 470).

It seems that, in spite of the reasons for distinguishing the idea that the axioms of set theory are forced on us from the idea that expansions of concepts are, Gödel would not have wanted to distinguish between the two.

Further evidence that the first argument can be understood in terms of the second can be found in Wang Hao's comment that Gödel qualified his argument about the perception of objects by saying that "it is like seeing from an airplane." The idea of seeing from afar is very similar to a remark made by Gödel with regard to the idea that concepts force themselves on us. Gödel's remark (in Wang 1996, p. 305) that the distinction between intuition *de dicto* and *de re* is not a sharp one, since each one is included in the other, suggests that we should not try to distinguish the way axioms and concepts are forced on us, even if this is not entailed by his comment. This also follows from the fact that the analysis of a concept reveals constraints on it that can be expressed as propositions.

The connection between the perception of a concept and the principles that apply to it is an internal one. Not only does the perception of a proposition have a necessary connection with the concepts used in the proposition, but understanding a concept makes use of the principles connected with it. If this is the case, then it is possible to hold that the axioms of set theory force themselves on us by seeing them as constraints on the concept of a set, which are revealed in the process of working with sets. In this respect the axioms of set theory are like the constraints on the concepts of measure and number.[13]

DISCUSSION

So far I have presented Gödel's second argument, and I hope I have succeeded in demonstrating its connection with the idea that concepts force themselves on us and the notion that concepts are perceived. The rest of the chapter will be devoted to examining the argument for the objective existence of concepts. First I will try to see if its underlying assumption is reasonable, that is, whether concepts really do force themselves on us. Afterwards I will examine the validity of the argument, that is, whether the conclusion that concepts exist indeed follows from this assumption.

---

[13] Ms. Hilly Rezinsky commented that I have not proved anything about the objects in set theory. Perhaps the connection between a concept and its extension can be used to go from the perception of concepts to the perception of the set constituting its extension. This would show that we can perceive at least some sets.

Gödel's claim that forced expansions are unique needs revision. In his view the system of basic laws that need to be conserved, which makes the expansion a forced one, is unique, and the way to expand concepts while preserving these laws is also unique. Apparently he was unaware of the possibility of forced expansions that are not strongly forced. A concrete example of this with respect to the continuum problem can be found in Gödel's essay, "What is Cantor's Continuum Problem?" (Gödel 1983a). As mentioned, this essay begins with the claim that the title question is meaningful only if the concept of number is expanded uniquely. Afterwards Gödel states that we have a strong requirement that the concept of the number of a set should be independent of the properties of its elements, such as color or weight. From this he deduces that there is only one way to expand the concept of number. Now Gödel was right in claiming that certain constraints force a unique expansion of the concept of number, but it is possible to choose other constraints that are no less natural and obtain a different definition of number. The fact that we are not forced to choose one particular expansion does not mean that the laws we find do not determine the concept of number. The concept's independence of the properties of the elements of the set is one requirement that does not determine the expansion, but there are other ways of expanding the concept of number that Gödel did not consider, and the very fact that they exist shows that the question does not have only one meaning. When we ask what the number of all the sets of natural numbers might be, we are not grasping a question that can be understood in a unique way.

This phenomenon also recurs in other expansions. Lebesgue's concept of measure survived a confrontation with other forced expansions. Yet the concept of measure or quantity can be expanded in other ways while preserving other laws. If, for example, σ-additivity is given up, then an expansion can be obtained in which all sets are measurable. It is true that the fruitfulness of Lebesgue's expansion justifies using the concept of measure he proposed, but it does not justify simply ignoring other non-arbitrary expansions. If we take into account the norms and other considerations that made these particular expansions so fruitful, then we can ask the following question about Gödel's claim: is it really true that the uniqueness of our expansions is a fact of mathematics?

Careful reflection shows that we do not have any a priori guarantee that this claim is true. In fact, it would be wrong to describe the process of expansion of concepts as a progression from a vague intuitive concept to a *unique* underlying concept. Indeed, the very example of Lebesgue's integral that Gödel cites (as quoted above) can serve as a counterexample to his own claim. There is no necessity that the norms which guide us in choosing a fruitful expansion will always pick out the same one. In the case of the expansion of the integral, the principle of choosing the expansion that preserves the largest number of laws and the principle of choosing the expansion that creates the largest number of distinctions pull us in different directions. Lebesgue's expansion preserves more laws, but leaves some sets immeasurable, while some other expansion might cover all sets but fail to preserve σ-additivity. This characteristic is not coincidental – there is always a trade-off between the range of application of some laws and the nature of the laws that are valid. The more we expand the range of application, the harder it is to preserve all the laws.

Like other logicians, Gödel was not sufficiently aware of this trade-off. What it entails is uncertainty – we can never be sure that we possess the best possible concept of number or the ultimate concept of measure. Moreover, we can never even be sure that there actually exists one concept that is absolutely the best. This uncertainty should not prevent us from continuing our search, of course, since it is always possible that what we thought was the end of the road is not actually that. The concepts we have are fruitful only relative to the knowledge in our possession, and there can be other, better concepts that are still out of our reach. We must therefore continue to suggest new expansions of concepts and investigate their implications, even if we cannot examine them immediately but must first gather more material in the form of proofs and additional expansions.

One possible reaction to this criticism would be to say that it refutes Gödel's arguments for realism and for the perception of concepts, since it refutes one of his assumptions – that a forced expansion leaves no room for choice. But this is not the only way of responding to the criticism.

I will begin with a simple way of rehabilitating Gödel's arguments. Even if there are several possible forced expansions, it may be possible to combine them in a broader picture. The concepts of measure and cardinal number, which can be combined as answers to the question "How much?" in the case of discrete finite groups, developed into two concepts which form a harmonious combination. This attempt to avoid the problem I raised above can be supported by Gödel's argument itself, since it claims, when we have only an intuitive concept, two different concepts can seem to be one, but when we sharpen our knowledge – which is equivalent to expanding our concepts – we may discover that there are actually two different concepts involved. Thus, even if there is more than one way of achieving sharp concepts, they are not achieved by an arbitrary choice, and the very fact that there exists a non-arbitrary expansion shows that the concepts really exist.

This emendation of Gödel's second argument weakens it somewhat, since it is based on the existence of a forced expansion rather than a unique concept that awaits us at the end of the development of a mathematical idea. Moreover, not every instance of the splitting of a concept by means of strongly forced expansions leads to two interesting concepts such as measure and number. Sometimes only one of the concepts proves interesting, as in Bernoulli's and Euler's expansions of the logarithm. Still, Gödel's argument can be amended by adding the claim that whenever there are several forced expansions, one of them is more natural than the others. But when there are two interesting forced expansions, as in the case of measure and cardinal number, then the power of each of the concepts and the connections between them are sufficient to allow us to claim that these are not only forced expansions but also products that have value beyond the process of expansion that led to them.

We can, however, suggest another attack on Gödel's position, in order to reduce the mystery involved in the very possibility of expanding a concept to one with sharper boundaries. This can be done by studying the genealogy of the number system. Mathematical objects are themselves the result of expansion, and therefore give us reason to expect that a function that is not defined everywhere can be defined on something that is seen as an expansion of its domain. This expectation may not always be satisfied, but that does not prevent it from being justified. The natural numbers are a product of repeatedly adding the unit. This makes it possible for many functions that are defined for some of the numbers to be expanded naturally to the rest. This is, after all, what happens in recursion – we have a function that is defined on some of the natural numbers and we make use of the structure of these numbers to define the function further. In order to see how likely this expectation is to be satisfied, we can compare the situation to what happens in cases of objects such that neither one is produced by the other. For example, a function that is defined for the earth's moon and oceans cannot be expanded to include the sun and the other stars, whereas a function that is defined on some of the numbers has a pre-drawn route for expansion which is derived from the internal relations among the numbers, relations that do not exist in the case of objects like stars and oceans.

Further examples of this idea can easily be found in expansions of functions that were defined on the natural numbers to include the negative numbers or the rational numbers, as well as in expansions from the rational numbers to the real numbers. A continuous expansion is generally guaranteed by the fact that the real numbers are precisely the expansion that makes the real numbers continuous. The way the real numbers are defined by means of the rational number – by Cauchy sequences, for example – provides a natural expansion for many of the functions that are defined on the rational numbers. We have a general principle which tells us that analytic functions are determined by their behavior on a small subset of the field of complex numbers. Two analytic functions which are identical on one convergent sequence are identical everywhere. It is due to this property of the number system that functions are determined uniquely, and so there is no reason to be surprised by the fact that we can begin with a concept that is defined on only part of a domain and end up with a concept defined on a larger domain.

Where certain expansions are concerned, however, it seems artificial to continue this line of attack on Gödel's argument. Consider, for example, the expansion of the factorial to fractions. Here it is very difficult to find a property that needs to be preserved in order to obtain a forced expansion, a property that invokes the global behavior of the function. But it is worth comparing the expansion of the factorial function from the rational numbers to the real numbers with the expansion of this function from the natural numbers to the rational numbers. The expansion from the rational numbers to the real numbers requires only the continuity of the function. The values of a continuous function are determined by its values for the rational numbers, for the reason given in the previous paragraph; since the real numbers were themselves obtained from the rational numbers by taking a certain closure, it is not very surprising that many expansions of functions that are defined on the rational numbers can be uniquely stretched to real numbers. The expansion of the factorial function from the natural numbers to the rational numbers, in contrast, does not follow the expansion of the natural numbers themselves to the rational numbers. The existence of such expansions as those for the factorial function is enough to retain some of Gödel's wonderment.[14]

At this point I would like to strengthen Gödel's argument even more. Not only does every expansion sharpen our concepts, but we can often

---

[14] Euler's expansion of the logarithm, which was based on the analysis of the Taylor series of the sine and cosine functions, and which pushed aside Bernoulli's algebraic expansion, is also relevant at this point. What we can learn from this is that sometimes an expansion that seems promising based on the way the domain was formed and the original meaning of the operations turns out not to be the best possible expansion.

obtain the same expansion in different ways. We created the complex numbers in order to provide an interpretation for expressions such as the square root of −1, or in order that every polynomial equation should have a solution, but they can also be obtained through the logarithmic function. The question of what power of 2 is −1 leads to the complex numbers in a different way from the algebraic question, but the end result is the same. The different ways of expanding the concepts or functions lead to the same number system. What could be more tempting than to claim that this system already existed before we discovered it?

So far I have examined the assumption underlying Gödel's second argument. Now I would like to examine the question of whether solving these problems with Gödel's assumption leads to realism concerning concepts. Gödel claims that the uniqueness of an expansion can be explained only if we assume that the outcome of the expansion was defined even before the expansion took place, and that the concepts already existed. But what exactly does it mean to say that a concept already existed or was already a sharp concept? Even if we agree that it is surprising that there are forced expansions and that they are uniquely determined, how does the assumption that the concepts already existed explain this? How can the addition of mathematical entities to a Platonic world explain this surprising phenomenon? Would it not be better to keep the mystery rather than trying to eliminate it by enriching our ontology?[15]

We have already seen the many analogies made by Gödel between what I have called progress in the tree of concept stages and the act of coming closer to a physical object that is unclear when viewed from afar. These analogies suggest formal qualities of what occurs in perception when we approach an object. Boundaries become sharper and can be used to understand what we saw before, and to answer questions that may have arisen, such as how the parts of the objects are arranged with respect to one another. We can also approach the object from various directions. Most importantly, the perception of the object is forced on us and is not dependent on our will.

Let us assume for the moment that progress in the tree of concept stages is analogous to sensory perception in all interesting respects, and that all the formal qualities of sensory perception are identical to those of the perception of concepts. In other words, let us assume that the strong

---

[15] A similar question can be asked of those who try to reduce the surprising nature of the applicability of mathematics to physics by taking a realistic position. Here too we can ask how the assumption that the mathematical concepts exist helps us explain their broad applicability.

interpretation suggested above is actually correct. Can we then explain how to validate Gödel's argument that mathematical concepts therefore exist the way physical objects do?

Here is one possibility. If the phenomenon of forced expansions of concepts is enough to lead us to the conclusion that concepts can be perceived, then we can try to deduce the existence of concepts from the fact that perception must be the perception of something, and thus that the appropriate candidate for the object of the perception is the concept. This requires a new explication of the idea of objective reality. We have to claim that the formal qualities of perception and their connection to what is grasped as the object of perception are part of the analysis of objective existence. It is not because we can focus on what we see and thus achieve a sharp picture that we deduce that there is something there. The meaning of the claim that "there exists" an object or a concept is the possibility of focusing in order to see more details and going from a vague situation to a sharp one (and maintaining the other analogies), and this possibility can be defined independently of the concept of sensory perception. Now, since the same formal qualities exist in the case of both physical and mathematical objects, at least to the extent that we understand the perception of concepts here through the argument from expansions, we can deduce that the objective status of mathematical objects is identical to that of physical objects. Thus the expansion of the concept of perception from material objects existing in time and space to entities independent of time and space results in an expansion of the concept of truth and objectivity in a way that makes them more abstract.

This idea can be illustrated by considering whether there is only one world of sets. The naive realist view holds that there is only one such world, which we are trying to investigate, and so there must finally be one set theory. If we accept what I claimed in the previous paragraph, then we can see that another picture is possible. We begin with a vague, intuitive concept of a set and gradually develop the principles that are supposed to apply to it, attempt to avoid contradictions, strive for the maximum number of sets, and the like. Assume that at a certain stage we see that there is only one way of developing set theory. This uniqueness can be turned into an argument for the existence of one set theory and one independent world of sets. Thus it is not because we believe that there is one world of sets independent of our theory that we believe that there is one set theory; on the contrary, the fact that set theories converge to one single theory supports the position that there is an objective concept of a set.

In sum, this chapter has had two different purposes. One was to provide an example of how a consideration of forced expansions can help us find this notion in the work of other philosophers. This kind of reflection may help us understand more clearly other issues in philosophy that appeal to the notion of expansion. Among them are the debate between Brouwer and Hilbert and the controversy between Dummett and Putnam mentioned at the end of chapter 1. The discussion in chapter 9 on the paradoxes exemplifies this strategy in another domain. The second purpose was to better understand what I called Gödel's second argument. In my interpretation Gödel presented a new view of the relevance of the nature of expansions for philosophical issues in mathematics. The perspective I have suggested here, it seems to me, enriches Gödel's argument and also invites several developments in the light of other suggestions presented above. Among these are comparing Wittgenstein's notion of family resemblance with Gödel's more essentialist view, comparing Gödel's and Frege's notions of what a concept is, and investigating the relation between forced expansions, formulated as $F(T, A)$, and the notion of perception, all of which are beyond the scope of this book.

Implications for thoughts

If the truth can be stretched, what does this tell us about the meanings of sentences? This question must arise in any approach that connects the meanings of sentences with the concept of truth. But, as we have seen again and again, Frege's position gives this question a unique significance. Frege distinguished between science and fiction, calling the latter a realm where sentences have meaning without having truth-value, or, more precisely, where it does not matter what the truth-value of a sentence might be. Stretching the truth thus entails refiguring the distinction between science and fiction. The possibility of such a refiguring does, however, have a favorable implication. Just as true sentences can be used in literature, because they may be interesting for reasons other than their truth-value, there can also be sentences which lack a reference in Frege's view, yet are worthy of scientific discussion because they may potentially have a truth-value.

I therefore suggest that it is worth distinguishing a set of inchoate thoughts within the world of thoughts. These are partial senses of sentences that may either develop into complete thoughts or be discovered to be meaningless as the result of a non-arbitrary expansion. If we want to take seriously the idea that truth can be stretched, then we must amend several basic laws of Frege's involving thoughts and judgments. Subsequently I hope to sharpen my view by comparing it with that of Wittgenstein, the only thinker I know of who expresses a similar opposition to Frege.

THREE FREGEAN PRINCIPLES

According to Frege, when a judgment is correct, it takes us from the grasp of a thought to the knowledge of its truth-value. As the result of such a judgment we are transformed from non-knowers into knowers. Nevertheless, this transformation does not involve the nature of the thought whose truth-value is at issue. This also implies that awareness of the reasons that led to the judgment about the truth-value of the sentence does not change the thoughts that we grasp. The question that arises here is how much of this picture can be preserved when we are deciding upon the truth-value of a sentence containing a concept that has undergone a forced expansion. This is a natural question because the principles that decide the truth-value of the thought are generally determined at the same time as the sense of the sentence in question. It is as if we create the content in the process of judging its truth-value. In the spirit of Wittgenstein's discussion of Cantor's proof of the non-denumerability of $\mathbb{R}$, we should understand the proposition "These considerations may lead us to say that $2^{\aleph_0} > \aleph_0$" as claiming that "We can *make* the considerations lead us to say that that $2^{\aleph_0} > \aleph_0$" (Wittgenstein 1967, p. 58).

Incorporating this intuition within the context of Frege's comments allows us to draw a more exact picture. The following passage from his late writing is an excellent way to start our discussion:

The very nature of a question demands a separation between the acts of grasping a sense and of judging. And since the sense of an interrogative sentence is always also inherent in the assertoric sentence that gives an answer to the question, this separation must be carried out for assertoric sentences too. It is a matter of what we take the word "thought" to mean. In any case, we need a short term for what can be the sense of an interrogative sentence. I call this a thought (Frege 1977b, p. 119).

Here Frege distinguishes between making a judgment and grasping the sense of a particular sentence by considering what happens when we ask a question. At the time that we are asking the question we are grasping something even before we have made a judgment, and this distinction between the grasp of a thought at the stage of asking "Is P true?" is transferred to the situation in which someone is thinking about P when she already has the answer. Later on I will analyze this claim explicitly, but even at this point it is clear how it fits into our discussion, since we are trying to show that when we answer certain questions by making forced expansions, we change the meaning of the answers.[1]

It is worth formulating Frege's argument for distinguishing between making judgments and grasping thoughts in order to expose some major assumptions in Frege's view. The first assumption that suggests itself is

---

[1] The question of whether this quotation fits Frege's thought in general, like the question about the coherence of what he is saying here, is of secondary importance in the present context.

that there is no development on the level of thoughts. Nothing develops into a thought, and a sentence either has or does not have a sense. Let us call this "Frege's first principle." The sense of a sentence is what the sentence says, and Frege's first principle is that there is no such thing as a sentence with "half a sense."[2] This principle was not explicitly formulated by Frege himself, but it seems basic to his view. As we shall see shortly, something like Frege's first principle is needed for proving Frege's assertion that when we answer a question we are *not* performing an operation on the thought involved. In order to demonstrate this, it is necessary to add two more principles. When we ask a question of the form "Is it true that P?" we are grasping something. The question precedes its answer, and many years may pass from the time the question is asked until it is answered. Moreover, the question may be transmitted from one person to another. In all these processes we are grasping thoughts. Frege, as shown above, is even prepared to define a thought as what we grasp when we ask a question of the form "Is it true that P?" Let us call this "Frege's second principle."

Frege's third principle, which can also be extracted from the passage cited above, states that what we grasp in a question is somehow inherent in the sense of the answer. This principle too is intuitively appealing. Without such a connection we could not say why the answer is an answer to this particular question rather than some other one. If the justification of the answer determined the sense of the question, it would be hard to see what could prevent us from answering the question arbitrarily, thus changing the meaning of the question so that the arbitrary answer becomes an appropriate answer to the question under its new meaning.

These three principles are needed for proving the proposition that judgment does not involve the sense of the question and that the sense of the question ("Is P true?") is identical with the sense of the answer ("P") rather than having some other form of connection with it. The argument proceeds as follows. When we ask a question we understand something (this is the second principle) and this something is included in the answer (according to the third principle). Now we can see the necessity of holding the first principle, as without it one could say that at the stage of the question we had grasped only part of what appeared in the answer. And since, according to this principle, a thought has no

---

[2] Obviously one does not have to be a Fregean or accept the world of thoughts as different from the world of objects and words in order to adopt this principle. Even if one believes that what is true or false is a sentence rather than a thought, one can claim that there are no half-sentences.

variations or degrees, what was grasped in the question is what is grasped in the answer.

Presenting Frege's argument in this way advances us considerably in our understanding of the implications of stretching the truth for issues of meaning. Since we suspect that forced expansions are connected with the sense of questions, as this is the conclusion of the above argument, we must try to deal with the principles that lead to this conclusion. Frege himself helps us locate the most problematic principle when he writes the following introduction to his previously cited definition of a thought:

A propositional question [*Satzfrage*] contains a demand that we should either acknowledge the truth of a thought, or reject it as false. In order that we may meet this demand correctly, two things are requisite: first, the wording of the question must enable us to recognize without any doubt the thought that is referred to; secondly, this thought must not belong to fiction (1977b, p. 117).

Here Frege presents the conditions for having a real question. The first condition is a requirement that the expression be unequivocal, while the second condition, as we know from other contexts in which Frege uses the term "fiction," is a requirement that every name must denote an object and every predicate must denote a concept defined unambiguously everywhere. This introduction raises several difficulties, the most important of which involves the point of these conditions. The definition in the paragraph that follows it (the one cited above), which presents a thought as what is grasped when one asks a question, implies that whatever is the content of a possible question is a thought. This characterization does not contain the slightest hint that we have to make sure that there is a real problem before we pose a question. In order for something to be a problem it is usually enough that one is thinking about it and trying to solve it. According to Frege's introduction, one must inspect the formulation and determine that there is indeed a thought here, and only afterwards seek its truth-value. If one must check to see that what one has is a thought in order to be able to ask a question, then there is no point in appealing to the intuition that whenever we ask a question we are grasping something, and calling that thing a thought.

This imprecision involves a problem that occupies an important place in commentaries on Frege on the possibility and status of senses without reference. The discussion here implies that there is no intuitive psychological difference between grasping the sense of fictional and scientific sentences. We can imagine that we are asking a question even if this is not the case, and it is for this reason that we must examine whether the combination of words used in the question satisfies the two requirements. Only after this has been done can we know whether we have a real question and therefore also a real thought.

THE SECOND PRINCIPLE EMENDED

This implies that Frege would have restricted the second principle in the following way: if the names in a question "Is it true that *P*?" denote objects, and if the predicates denote concepts that are defined everywhere, then when we try to find out whether *P* is the case, we are indeed asking a question and grasping something; otherwise we are not.

This restriction leads us to the heart of the subject matter of the present chapter. There may be agreement that the expression "When was Hamlet born?" – or, to put it as a yes-or-no question, "Was Hamlet born in 1750?" – does not denote a question if Hamlet never existed. The expression "Hamlet was born in 1977" is senseless, at least as far as science is concerned, if "Hamlet" does not denote a living creature, and so it may be claimed that it is not part of the language of science. But the case of incomplete predicates, or predicates that are not defined on a given object, is a different matter. The expressions "What is the logarithm of -1?" or "What is the temperature inside a black hole?" or "What is the age of the universe?" are questions even if we do not assume that the black holes possess a well-determined temperature and the universe a well-determined age.

If someone asks, "When was Hamlet born?" we can say, "Don't you realize that 'Hamlet' is a fictional character?," but if a scientist asks about the age of the universe or the temperature of a black hole or log(-1), we do not say, "Don't you realize that the functions you are talking about are not defined for those cases?" If we had to judge such expressions according to Frege's view, then we could be sure they were actually questions only if we knew that the concept of age is defined for everything in the world, including the universe itself, or that the concept of temperature is defined for everything in the world, including black holes. Only then could we describe the utterance of such expressions as asking a question. But if the concept of temperature were already defined for black holes, this would take away the whole point of our question.

Moreover, it is not clear how Frege's demand could be satisfied. In order to ask "Is *A* a *T*?," according to Frege, we must first check to see if

A is an object, which at this point we can put to one side as unproblematic, and then we must also check to see if *T* is defined everywhere, but how can we do that?[3] And would not such a check, in the case where we do not know the answer, be equivalent to checking whether "Is *A* a *T*?" is a meaningful question? If this is so, then the restriction Frege is trying to place on the second principle is worthless.[4]

Since Frege did not distinguish questions such as "Was Hamlet a birdwatcher?" from questions that can only be answered by means of a forced expansion, and therefore must involve concepts that are not defined everywhere, we must amend Frege's second principle. Questions such as "Is $2^{-1} > 1$?" do not involve fiction, even though the predicate is undefined. Nevertheless, I am not claiming that such questions are purely ordinary ones, nor that it could not turn out after investigation that a question of this sort is meaningless. Thus I am not trying to blur the important distinction made in recent Fregean interpretation between cases where it seems to me that I am thinking and cases where I am really thinking. I would like, however, to broaden Frege's second principle so that it applies to such questions as well. The revised principle states that when we ask a question which can be answered by means of a forced expansion, then we grasp something that I am calling an inchoate thought.

Inchoate thoughts

We began with a vague intuition that a forced expansion of a concept contributes to the meaning of sentences in which it occurs. The discussion of Frege's principles now allows us to sharpen this intuition to create a more precise picture. All we have to do is examine the relation between what is said by a sentence that denotes a thought – that is, what is true or false – and what we grasp when we ask a question whose answer is given

---

[3] And what if the predicate is defined for *A* but not for some other *B*? Can we ask the question in such a case? This is another clear sense in which there is a lack of analogy between the case of predicates that are not defined everywhere and the case of names without reference.

[4] Diamond's interpretation can provide us with an answer to this last question. Diamond claims that Frege is not offering an internal criterion for deciding whether an expression denotes a thought. You can ask or not ask a question, grasp or not grasp a thought, without being certain that you are indeed thinking a thought. If the expressions denote what they are supposed to, then you really have a thought, otherwise not. This emendation does not eliminate the transparency of the thought, since you can know *what* you are thinking even though you generally cannot know *that* you are thinking. Total definability of the concepts is required to guarantee that you are indeed thinking, but the purpose of this requirement is not to provide an internal test for deciding whether you are thinking, and so you are not expected to actually perform the test to find out whether the concepts are indeed defined everywhere. This way of saving Frege, however, has the effect of rendering logic a hypothetical science (see next chapter).

by a forced expansion – that is, what is potentially true or false. This expression leads us to Frege's first principle. The existence of inchoate thoughts makes it necessary to amend this principle. We must say that if a sentence expresses an inchoate thought, then its sense is not complete, since it may be given additional determinations that will then complete it. A sentence that expresses an inchoate thought is neither true nor false, but its sense can be developed by a forced expansion so as to make it true or false.

There is no need to change the third principle for this purpose. An inchoate thought exists within the thought into which it is developing. We can therefore use Frege's terminology (from the passage quoted above) to say that a sentence expressing an inchoate thought is inherent in a sentence whose truth-value is determined. We retain the intuition on which the third principle is based, since it is clear that even if the sense of the sentence whose truth-value is determined after the expansion is not identical with what we grasped at first, it is still not possible to give just any answer to the question we posed. The only acceptable answers are those in which the inchoate sense develops into a complete sense.

This is the picture in a nutshell, but now it must be extended and qualified.

First we must consider the very expression "inchoate thoughts." When I describe a situation in which an inchoate thought develops into a complete thought, I do not describe it as if there were two independent thoughts that are different from each other. If this were the case, then we would have to say that a sentence that had expressed a thought which had been classified as fiction or that had not expressed a thought at all was now given a new sense. But such a formulation would not capture the fact that there is a transition here from one sense to another, and that this transition is an essential, systematizable component of mathematical and scientific methodology. Just as we have already refuted the notion that the stages of a concept are distinct concepts, we must also reject the claim that two different senses are being attributed to the same sentence.

In general, what is involved here is not an ambiguous sentence with two similar meanings, nor a sentence which sometimes has a meaning that belongs to fiction and at other times denotes a scientific proposition. We can imagine that archeological discoveries, like Schliemann's discovery of ancient Troy, would provide evidence that sentences which we thought belonged to the realm of fiction are actually propositions about the real world. Thus, for example, while we now think that the sentence "Odysseus was not a Trojan" is merely part of a fictional Homeric tale, and that "Odysseus" is an expression with sense but no reference, further archeological evidence could bring us to believe that there may actually have been such a person as "Odysseus," just as we now know that there was such a place as Troy. In such a case the sentence would have a scientific sense and a reference.

But even if we describe such a possible situation as providing a new meaning for "Odysseus," in addition to the legendary meaning, we would still need to distinguish this situation from the one where "the square root of -1" obtained a new meaning when we expanded the system of real numbers into the system of complex numbers. For this expansion was obtained, at least according to my description in chapter 6, from the sense that "the square root of -1" had before the expansion, whereas "Odysseus" might not obtain its new sense directly from the sense it had in the legend.

This point is even clearer when we consider "$\log(-1)$," whose new reference did not require expanding our ontology. Even though it was because of the legend that we were able to discover Troy, we still do not say that "Odysseus" was given a reference through the legend. On the contrary, we might say that "Odysseus" always denoted a person even though we did not know it. The sense of "$\log(-1)$," however, developed out of the previous sense, and this justifies our claim that the earlier sense was an inchoate one.

It is possible to be so impressed with the similarity between the sense of "$\log(-1)$" before and after the expansion as to claim that there is really only one sense involved, rather than the development of an inchoate sense into a complete one. But this would be to claim much more than is admissible, because a sense that is not associated with a reference, such as "$\log(-1)$" before the expansion, cannot be the same as a sense that does have a reference.

It is therefore worth offering an additional argument based on the phenomenon of forced expansions that are not strongly forced. We begin with the statement that no question with a well-determined sense can have two different incompatible correct answers. This is a result of Frege's tenet: if the sense of a correct answer is the same as the sense of the question it is answering, then a question with two incompatible correct answers would have two different senses. Therefore, when we encounter a question that is answered through a forced expansion that is not strongly forced, we should see its meaning not as complete but as inchoate.

When we ask a question, whether an inchoate one or an ordinary one, we are grasping something. What we grasp in the case of an inchoate question is no less objective than the content of a normal question. Moreover, the content of an inchoate question is not veiled (there is nothing behind it), but is completely transparent to the thinker. An inchoate question is fully grasped, yet the *content* that is grasped may go through some changes.

It is also easy to distinguish between inchoate thoughts and ambiguous sentences in which the plurality of meanings is given at the outset. When we claim that in some sense a proposed answer is true we do not render the thought entertained at the stage of asking a question ambiguous, at least not in the way that "Did you go to the bank?" is ambiguous. For the possible compilations of an inchoate thought are not normally given at the moment of asking the question, but appear only after we find incompatible ways of answering it. Moreover, even after discovering two different meanings we can never know what new meanings will be revealed as a result of future study. If we have an ambiguity here, then it is always potential and open-ended.

There is a difference between a sentence about which we do not know if it denotes a thought or not and one that expresses an inchoate thought. Wittgenstein brings an interesting example of someone who asks, "Does the number of pages in my notebook solve the equation A?" when he does not know if equation A has a solution. In such a case I would not claim that the questioner was grasping an inchoate thought. Rather, he was either grasping an ordinary thought, if the equation actually has a unique solution, or he was not grasping a thought at all, if the equation has no solution. In either case there are no inchoate thoughts involved, even if the speaker thought he was grasping something when he asked the question.

It is thus clear that I am not extending Frege's second principle to include the claim that whenever it seems to you that you have asked a question you are actually grasping something. Yet forced expansions allow us to provide a richer picture of what happens when we discover that a question is meaningless. When it turns out that after a forced expansion an expression becomes meaningless, then I do not claim that what I grasped at the stage of asking the question was meaningless at that time, but rather that the forced answer "caused" its inchoate meaning to be "aborted," that is, it "caused" the expression to develop in a direction that led it to become meaningless. But this development is not necessarily the end of the road, since, in cases where the forced expansion leading to the meaninglessness of the expression is not strongly forced, as generally occurs, it is still possible that some other forced expansion will ascribe a meaning to the expression. This is especially important when we are trying to prove that some expression is meaningless. Kant thought he had proved that the question about the age of the universe is meaningless, but the new cosmologists have found a way of formulating the question so as to give it a meaning. This topic, which touches on the general question of the nature of metaphysical questions, is discussed in detail in the next chapter.

We are now in a position to be more precise in our discussion of the way our justification of a forced expansion contributes to the sense of the answer. When we ask an inchoate question we do not know what constraints we will have to use in order to force the answer. Thus, when we provide an answer, the constraints we have chosen do not constitute assumptions that would have been valid for the new case if there were no expansion involved, but rather the extension of a law to an instance for which it was not known whether it would be valid. When we encounter an answer to an inchoate question, we must look for the laws that forced the expansion which made the answer possible. Such laws are necessary not only to provide grounds for the answer, but also to show us *how* to understand it. This is also the reason that Frege's distinction between thinking and judging is not a sharp one in the case of inchoate questions.

Let me conclude this section by noting that in a static situation there is no point talking about inchoate thoughts, at least not in the sense that I am using. In a particular model with clear laws the question of what $2^{2^i} + 2$ equals is either undefined within this model or, if it is defined within the model, then the question is answered according to the way it is defined. In either case, however, there is no inchoate question here. Only when we want to provide laws in order to force a meaning and not merely to decide a question – in other words, only when we allow ourselves to go beyond the model, not seeing it as a final state, or when having no model at all, as is the case when we ask a question in a natural language – can we ask an inchoate question.

A REMARK ON WITTGENSTEIN

Among post-Fregean philosophers, Wittgenstein is the most prominent one to explicitly question the distinction between judging or justifying a statement and the statement's content.[5] Indeed, when he tells us that the best way of knowing what has been proven is to look at the proof, and

---

[5] The typical anti-realist, who connects the meaning of a sentence with the conditions for asserting it, is generally not committed to the claim that we shape the meaning of a sentence when we prove it.

that without the proof we cannot know what the proposition asserts, he is rejecting the Fregean picture, especially Frege's first principle. I do not intend to interpret Wittgenstein here, but only to use his views to sharpen my own position, which I have hitherto presented only in contrast with Frege's picture; it seems important to compare my view with one that is in opposition to Frege's as well.

Wittgenstein writes about expansions in many places, probably in different senses. I do not intend to list all these places, but it is worth mentioning some of the most prominent ones. Wittgenstein's reflections on extending a sequence according to a law, which he calls "following a rule" – in which each step is a leap in the dark – are especially important for the present purpose. His claim that calculating the arithmetic functions for large numbers may be an expansion or a change of the language is a somewhat different example, but the problems it highlights are similar to those presented in the passages on following a rule. Wittgenstein's comment that every calculation of a new number in the decimal expansion of π is an expansion of mathematics is meant to exemplify a group of similar expansions. In addition, the expression "It is five o'clock on the sun," which is discussed by Wittgenstein, is an example of an interesting expansion with implications for Wittgenstein's major ideas (Wittgenstein 1953, sec. 350).[6] These and other examples attest to Wittgenstein's great interest in expansions.

Wittgenstein did not, however, present any theory of expansions. He was interested in them in connection with other issues that he considered more important, such as the possibility of a private language and the picture theory. The way in which proofs force themselves upon us was indeed a major interest of Wittgenstein's, and here and there he offers an illuminating example that is relevant to the topic of expansions. Even his discussion of "family resemblance" is intended to explain why he is not obliged to offer a definition for words like "game." But even though Wittgenstein did not have a theory of expansions, we can gain a great deal from those of his discussions that are connected with this issue. Indeed, Wittgenstein's examples are capable of throwing cold water on any logician who aspires to a general theory of the essence of expansions.

The discussion here, however, will be limited to Wittgenstein's thesis that it is the proof of a proposition that gives it its sense. Here is a typical passage where he expresses this view:

---

[6] On this point I refer the reader to Kripke's (1982, pp. 117–21) discussion of this example.

It seems that it is only when we have the answer that we know how to understand the question. Before the proof "there was only a rough pattern of the sense in the verbal language" – and the idea that it might in some way be filled in, the expression given mathematical sense (Wittgenstein 1967, p. 153).

But even if we limit ourselves to this particular aspect of Wittgenstein's thought, his notion of the way a proof shapes the meaning of a proposition is not unambiguous. First of all, its extent is not clear. Does every proof shape the meaning of what has been proven? Do even short, two-line proofs using modus ponens change the meaning of what they prove? To give an even more extreme example, does the transition from $P \& Q$ to P change the meaning of P? Or is it only proofs of propositions in the foundations of mathematics that shape the meaning of what has been proven?[7] Wittgenstein claims that a proof modifies concepts, yet he insists that he does not have an unambiguous notion of what a concept is. In fact, his use of the word "concept" is rather odd. He asks, for example, "Is the conceptual apparatus a concept?"(Wittgenstein 1967, IV 45) and "Is not the new concept the proof itself?" (ibid.). He even admits that "the word 'concept' is by far too vague" (V 39).

One articulation of Wittgenstein's position is to see it as directed at foundational issues in mathematics. In an analogy that has been much discussed, especially by Diamond, Wittgenstein explains what is involved in these issues:

Like the problem set by the king in the fairy tale who told the princess to come neither naked nor dressed, and she came wearing fishnet ... He didn't really know what he wanted her to do, but when she came thus he was forced to accept it. It was of the form "Do something which I shall be inclined to call neither naked nor dressed." It's the same with mathematical problems, "Do something which I shall be inclined to accept as a solution, though I don't know now what it will be like" (quoted from Diamond, 1995, p. 267).

The connection between this description and what was presented earlier in this chapter is clear. Wittgenstein does not think that when we answer a mathematical question we provide a ready-made answer, the way we do when we answer a question such as, "How many people are there in the room?" Whether I am merely inclined or actually forced to accept the answer when it appears, the sense of the question was not definite at the time it was asked.

---

[7] There is also a third alternative – that there is a conceptual change involved in the very acceptance of the entire sequence of steps that embodies a proof (Wittgenstein 1967, I 33).

Now, I cannot do justice here to the depth, complexity, and multiplicity of meanings in Wittgenstein's approach. But if we look at one of the views that can be extracted from this complex (which may be called Wittgenstein I), we can find several interesting distinctions. The most fundamental distinction involves the word "inclined," as it appears in Wittgenstein's remarks. The use of this word is not coincidental, as can be seen by comparing a genuine mathematical problem with a riddle such as "Kiss your ear!" The condition for a good solution to this riddle, like that of the solution involving the fishnet, is our inclination to accept it as such, which may be shared with many of the members of our community, but it is still no more than an inclination. However, the proof that angle trisection by classical means is impossible, as well as the proof that there are different kinds of infinities, are supposed to be understood like the command to kiss one's own ear. In such cases Wittgenstein agrees that the transition is not arbitrary, since we have to suggest something that we are inclined to see as a solution to the problem, but this non-arbitrariness is no more well founded than linguistic analogies.

This description implies that our creation and acceptance of linguistic analogies are based on a human tendency. If we interpret Wittgenstein this way, then we can distinguish between his view and what has been said here about forced expansions, since these involve more than a mere tendency to accept them. In this sense the difference between Wittgenstein's view and the one presented here is the difference between the idea of family resemblance, as described in the previous chapter, and the notion of concept stages. Expansions have too strong a normativity to be considered mere tendencies. Indeed, as I explained in chapter 1, when mathematicians in the seventeenth and eighteenth centuries accepted the expansions that were proposed then, they clearly had no prior tendency to accept them. The reaction to them was mixed, to say the least: some members of the mathematical community, such as Euler, accepted them, while others, such as Pascal, did not, and the rest, including Leibniz, were ambivalent about them. Sometimes we do have a tendency to accept an expansion, but there is something in expansions that is independent of our tendencies.

If we want to criticize Frege's position, it is worth considering the suggestion that what we find in the case of mathematical problems is what we find in riddles. I agree with the following remarks of Wittgenstein about Cantor: "The dangerous, deceptive thing about the idea: 'The real numbers cannot be arranged in series,' or again 'The set . . . is not denumerable' resides in its making what is a determination, formation, of a concept look a fact of nature" (1967, p. 56). Indeed, in forced expansions as well we do not necessarily find some truth that has been hidden somewhere – if we leave Gödel's argument aside for the moment. But even if we admit that there is no revelation of some fixed, a priori truth involved here, it would be a mistake to conclude that expansions and all the theorems that have been deduced from them are merely based on analogy, like the answer to the riddle about being neither dressed nor naked or understanding the order "Kiss your ear!" Here we must say that Wittgenstein offered a comparison in order to criticize Frege's picture, but this comparison must be amended because it is liable to lead to another picture which, although perhaps less problematic than Frege's, remains inappropriate for the case of mathematics, in which there is a systematicity that does not exist in Wittgenstein's analogies. Even though the sense is not determined at the time the question is asked, there is a fairly concrete methodology that constrains expansions, making them normative procedures.

In general, even though there is a connection between inchoate thoughts and riddles whose solutions we can recognize when we see them, as well as between these two on the one hand and analogies and metaphors on the other, it is still worth maintaining the distinctions between all these notions, especially in attempting to see what each of them can teach us about the others. There is no a priori guarantee that the ways in which words are taken beyond their ordinary meanings can be systematically classified. We must therefore keep in mind that even though the most important issue in mathematical logic at present, which involves the number of points on a line, may be similar to some types of riddles, this similarity is not enough to enable us to fully understand the mathematical issue. If we compare it to the question of what $\log(-1)$ could be, then we can obtain another viewpoint which may lead us in the direction of the truth.

A sentence can lack a truth-value, yet its relations to other sentences can help us give it a definite meaning. This meaning depends on the terms that appear in the sentence and their occurrence in other sentences which do have a truth-value and a definite meaning. The conclusion of this chapter should be compared with Diamond's rejection of the idea of predicates that are not defined everywhere, which we met in chapter 2. Diamond claims that the ascription of a truth-value to sentences for which this value was not previously defined gives the sentence a meaning all at once, and that such a sentence cannot be decomposed into elements. But even if the present discussion has taken a somewhat holistic direction, since I claim that the new sense of the sentence is supported by constraints existing throughout the system, we still do not have to claim that this prevents us from analyzing language. Words have the property of resonating in every well-formed sentence in which they appear, and can endow such sentences with meaning as well. This property of words should be respected and not marginalized because of some particular theory of logical analysis.

Frege distinguished between fiction and science, seeing a great gap between them. The notion of inchoate thoughts shows that what at first seems to belong to fiction may turn out in the end to belong to science. Wittgenstein's approach is liable to lead to the conclusion that some things that actually belong to science are fiction. When he compares mathematical questions to such a question as how many teeth Hamlet had, which can be decided arbitrarily by the author of the fictional work, this can be seen as an argument against Frege: "You think that mathematical questions are a matter of knowledge, in the same way as scientific facts, but this is not so." When Wittgenstein claims that Cantor misled us into thinking that what is only the creation of a concept is actually a fact of Nature, we are liable to see this as a sharp distinction between Nature and the idea of creating a concept, a distinction that is indefensible. This is not only because Nature itself, as I suggested in chapter 4, is sensitive to expansions, but because even something that does not describe facts or relations between facts can nevertheless be of crucial importance to our understanding of the world of facts.

Let me add that by admitting inchoate thoughts and at the same time allowing logic to study the process of stretching truths, we are not merely expanding logic but questioning Frege's confining it to the study of reference. Logic, for Frege, has no interest whatsoever in the senses of sentences:

[The intensionalist] logicians forget that the laws of logic are first and foremost laws in the realms of meanings [*Bedeutung*] and only relate indirectly to sense. If it is a question of the truth of something – and truth is the goal of logic – we also have to inquire after meanings; we have to throw aside proper names that do not designate or name an object, though they may have a sense . . . It must be determined for every object whether it falls under a concept or not . . . And for fiction the sense is enough . . . but not for science (Frege 1979, p. 122).

The passage from an inchoate thought to a thought entails the creation of a new sentence that carries a truth-value. The ability to understand such passages takes logic beyond the study of truth and expands it to include the constitution of truth.

"I was led astray by language"

The weird problems discussed by philosophers and the paradoxes encountered in philosophical discourse have often been connected with
the expansion of concepts. As I mentioned in chapter 1, this idea was
forcefully expressed by Kant, who considered the problems of dogmatic
metaphysics to be the result of the incautious expansion of concepts.
Questions about the cause of the world or the age of the universe come
from expansions of the concepts of cause and age which are valid for what
can be perceived by intuition – beyond what can be considered as phenomena, leading to illusions. We saw a variation of this view in the twen-
tieth century in the wake of the crisis in the foundations of mathematics.
Here too leading philosophers and logicians made remarks reminiscent
of Kant's position. The most prominent was Russell, who suggested, in
his theory of types, that Russell's paradox can be dealt with by avoiding
the claim that all properties are meaningful for all objects. This analysis,
like Kant's, asserts that we become involved in antinomies when we try
to expand our concepts to where they are not applicable (see, for example, the first page of the first edition of the first *Critique*). This move
has had a number of variations, some of which I present below. In fact,
remnants of this view guide various projects in the foundations of mathematics, including that of ZFC (Zermelo–Fraenkel and the axiom of
choice).

In this chapter I would like to examine this diagnosis of the phenomenon of paradoxes in light of the distinction between ordinary
thoughts and inchoate thoughts that I presented in the previous chapter.
The main topic of this chapter is how to go beyond Kant's and Russell's
views. I shall claim that the very attempt to find a clear dividing line
between acceptable expressions that do not lead to paradoxes, on the
one hand, and unacceptable, paradox-laden expressions, on the other,
stems from a misunderstanding of the logic of human language. It is not
the case that there is an unambiguous answer to the question of whether

the expression "the set of all sets" denotes an object or not, so that the task of the logician is merely to discover the correct answer to this question. Rather, the sentence "There is a set that includes all sets" should be seen as denoting an inchoate thought, that is, a thought on which we are trying to force a truth-value rather than discover one in some Platonic universe. As such, it is neither completely meaningful nor completely meaningless.

This chapter will also discuss Frege's reaction to Russell's paradox. Late in his life Frege expressed his pessimism about the possibility of constructing a valid logic, due to the impossibility of delineating a sharp boundary between expressions with a reference and those without one. His pessimism was based on his rigid requirement that logic cannot be studied properly without a notation that guarantees a reference for every name and predicate. I will try to discover what was bothering Frege and see whether my suggestions in this book could have helped him in any way.

THE DICHOTOMY PICTURE

According to the dichotomy picture (DP) there is a clear distinction between two types of expressions: those that are meaningful (or legitimate or acceptable) and those that are not.

I prefer to call this a picture rather than a theory, not only because, as we shall see, there are many variations of the DP, but also because I intend to deal with it only insofar as it involves paradoxes, without going into the type of meaning – or meaninglessness – that it is committed to.

Generally, an unacceptable sentence is one that has passed the test of being a sentence because its form is similar to that of other sentences in our language, but turns out upon examination to be misleading. This type of sentence can be a paradox, such as "This sentence is false," or a semantically odd sentence, such as "Bananas are honest," or any other sort of sentence to which we cannot easily assign a truth-value. When we become aware of this problem we say, "Our language has misled us."

The claim that there is an unambiguous distinction between meaningful and meaningless sentences generally leads to a demand for a criterion for making this distinction. This can be called the demarcation problem. Such a demand presupposes a realistic view of the issue, since its proponents are asserting that such a demarcation exists even though they do not yet know how to mark the boundary. Several philosophical projects were undertaken with the aim of delineating it. Let me mention a few.

At the beginning of this chapter I mentioned Kant's project of offering a criterion for the distinction between dogmatic and critical metaphysics, and I indicated that Russell's theory of types is another project of this sort. There is also the positivist principle associating meaning with the possibility of verification. According to the positivists the classification of sentences into meaningful and meaningless ones is co-extensive with classifying them into verifiable and unverifiable sentences. Yet we can claim that there is a distinction between meaningful and meaningless sentences while denying the possibility of finding a criterion for distinguishing them. This claim may be supported by a formal mathematical result – the reduction of the demarcation problem to formal undecidability. The claim that demarcation is impossible is also supported by the apparent intangibility of such a criterion. Wittgenstein concludes the *Tractatus* with the statement that "when someone else wished to say something metaphysical, to demonstrate to him that he had given no meaning to certain signs in his proposition" (Wittgenstein 1988, 6.53), I do not believe he is saying that there is a proven method for judging when a statement is acceptable and when it is not.

Placing a set of expressions in the category of illegitimate or meaningless ones does not necessarily entail that we have to exclude them from our language. In Zermelo–Fraenkel's theory of sets, we do not say that some expressions are meaningless. Rather, we divide all expressions into those that denote sets and those that denote classes which are not sets. The laws of naive set theory are valid only for real sets. As for classes, many people believe that we can live with them without getting involved in paradoxes, and without the need for declaring certain expressions meaningless. Even this solution, however, asserts that there is a distinction between expressions in one category and those in another; for example, we cannot quantify over classes. Thus some of the notion of meaninglessness still remains, and so this suggestion may also be viewed as a variation of the DP.

In the course of the history of philosophy, paradoxes and antinomies have been used as evidence for the DP claim. Kant believed that the existence of antinomies demonstrates that the categories have a limited domain of application, and we should not inquire about the cause or age of the world. In our terminology we would say that the expression "Age(World)," which is viewed here as applying a function Age(x) to the world, is problematic. Russell develops, on the basis of the paradoxes, a theory of types that requires considering such expressions as "$X \in X$" to be illegitimate.[1]

The DP is generally associated with the claim that the principles of logic, or the axioms we accept intuitively, have a clear range of applicability, being valid only up to a certain point. The claim that every sentence is either true or false, or that the universe must have either a finite or an infinite age, or that every property defines a set, or that every object either belongs to some set or does not belong to it, are claims that we considered to be absolutely and universally true until we discovered the antinomies. Here too we say that when we evaluated these claims we were misled by our reason or our intuition.

The claim that certain principles have led us astray, however, does not necessarily entail that illusion is involved here, nor does it entail the unambiguous dichotomy claim. The case of non-Euclidean geometry is undoubtedly one of the most important scientific revolutions that changed our epistemology as well, but we do not say that Euclidean geometry was an illusion. When we are faced with paradoxes and the failure of some of our generalizations, it is natural to claim that the problem is the meaninglessness of certain sentences. This is how Gödel described the problem in his critical remarks on Russell's theory of types:

It is not impossible that the idea of limited ranges of significance could be carried out without the above restrictive principle. It might even turn out that it is possible to assume every concept to be significant everywhere except for certain "singular points" or "limiting cases," so that the paradoxes would appear as something analogous to dividing by zero (1983b, p. 466).

Later on he states:

Such a system would be most satisfactory in the following respect: our logical intuitions would then remain correct up to certain minor corrections, i.e., they could then be considered to give an essentially correct, only somewhat "blurred," picture of the real state of affairs (1983b, p. 467).

What Gödel's remarks imply is something like this: we begin with self-evident principles, yet we end up with a contradiction. Nevertheless, we cannot make use of this contradiction to show that one of the principles

---

[1] An illegitimate expression may also be viewed as one that has no reference (see van Frassen 1978). In this case we can see it as an undefined point: if $F(\ )$ is the function that ascribes to each predicate its own extension, then $F("x \in x")$ does not denote any object. Nevertheless, in this chapter I am studying a picture, not a strict theory. I am therefore not supposing that all problems with illegitimate expressions belong to one type.

is false. If we could do this we would have a *reductio ad absurdum* proof of the negation of this principle, rather than a paradox. At this point we begin to consider the possibility that something in the expression at issue is problematic. This certainly does seem to be the case with expressions such as "This sentence is false," or "the universe," or "the set of all sets." It seems that, even though our logical principles are fundamentally sound, they do not apply to these problematic expressions.

A CRITIQUE OF THE DP

The category of sentences that refer to inchoate expressions, which I proposed in the previous chapter, raises the possibility that the DP is too simplistic. Indeed, the propositions that express inchoate, embryonic thoughts are neither meaningful nor meaningless. If my arguments for acknowledging this category are valid, then the DP position is problematic, and in fact we have the beginnings of a different position with regard to the foundation of mathematics. Recall the problem we are facing here. I do not intend to propose a formalism by which this or that paradox can be prevented. The DP has a respectable lineage, and demands that we search for the demarcation between types of expressions. It blames careless expansions of our laws over some expressions for creating paradoxes. Taking into account the argument of this chapter would suggest that perhaps there is no need to find the correct demarcation, or a different way of understanding paradoxes. As a result we can view attempts of proposing a division between meaningful and meaningless expressions from a different angle: one that brings them close to introducing a forced expansion.

However, it is insufficient to merely suggest this possibility. I will therefore try to show how it offers us the promises of a better picture. I would like to make it clear that this alternative is not the final word on the subject of paradoxes; at this stage it undoubtedly requires further development. But I do believe that it allows for a better assessment of paradoxes than the DP does.

One problem with the DP is that it does not provide a plausible account of the illusions involved in paradoxes. When we hold this view, we see ourselves as being mistaken in a fairly ordinary way, as if we had held a particular proposition and then discovered that the opposite is true. But the most basic phenomenological analysis shows that there is a difference between the mistake of dividing by zero and the illusion in believing that the expression "the set of all sets" denotes an object.

Gödel seems to be well aware of this problem, and he adds the following note:

Is the word "misunderstanding" appropriate for the characterization of the extensional paradoxes? Maybe we should call them oversight and mistaken application. Oversight is a more definite concept, but it is too light. Perhaps we should say persistent or serious oversight (quoted from Wang 1996, p. 273).

I fully agree with Gödel's intuition, but it is not easy to understand. One way of interpreting Gödel's expression of "persistent oversight" is in psychological terms. When a paradox is involved we make the sort of error that we have a psychological tendency to make. This is not an ordinary error in the sense of believing a certain proposition when the opposite is actually true, but an error caused by a tendency to err in this way.

Another way of understanding the difference between illusions and errors is Kant's classic discussion of this issue in his view of metaphysical illusions, which locates the source of our errors in the nature of human reason:

Logical illusion, which consists merely in the imitation of the form of reason (the illusion in sophistical syllogisms), arises entirely from a want of due attention to logical rules. So soon as the attention is awakened to the case before us, this illusion totally disappears. Transcendental illusion, on the contrary, does not cease to exist even after it has been exposed ... Take, for example, the illusion in the proposition: "The world must have a beginning in time" ... There is therefore a natural and unavoidable dialectic of pure reason – not that in which the bungler, from want of requisite knowledge, involves himself, nor which the sophist devises for the purpose of misleading, but that which is an inseparable adjunct of human reason, and which, even after its illusions have been exposed, does not cease to deceive (Kant 1933, A-297, B-353).

For Kant, in contrast to Gödel, analyzing an illusion does not show that it is a mere psychological tendency, but rather demonstrates that it stems from reason itself (that is why he called his book *Critique of Pure Reason*).[2]

But both analyses of the distinction between an illusion and an accidental mistake arise naturally out of the DP position, and I believe that in the final analysis neither of them is satisfactory. To say about

---

[2] There is another difference between Kant and Gödel that should not be dismissed: Kant does not discuss set theory paradoxes, while Gödel's remark above deals only with set theory, and not with intentional paradoxes (such as a concept not applying to itself). Gödel thought that "for concepts the paradoxes point to bankruptcy, but for sets they are misunderstandings" (Wang 1996, p. 273).

illusions in set theory that they stem from a psychological tendency (such as occurs when someone thinks that anyone on the other side of the earth must fall off, or the common mistake in removing parentheses, setting $a - (b - c) = a - b - c$ is not enough. Yet to say that the source of illusion is reason seems incoherent. Would it not be better to ascribe to reason the role of leading us to the truth, and to say that if anything leads us to illusion, then it must be our imagination? This question was raised in Kant's time by Solomon Maimon, and was later posed by Frege. (In the next section I will discuss this further.) It seems that anyone who says that illusions stem from reason is trying to express the intuition that what we have here is more than psychology, but cannot find the right way of saying it without creating a new problem.

To sharpen the distinction between a mistake and an illusion, it would be helpful to look at the following problem: the DP assumes there is only one way of sorting expressions into meaningful and meaningless ones, but there may be different possible set theories that can resolve the paradox while disagreeing about the categorization of expressions. When we discover a paradox, we know that something is wrong, but what makes us think that whatever is wrong can be located in one single way?

The problem of what makes an expression acceptable cannot be solved separately. If we consider the various suggested solutions for the problem raised by the paradoxes, we can see that they disagree on both the diagnosis of the problem and the classification of the expressions into meaningful and meaningless ones.[3]

The fact that the set of all sets belongs to itself violates the axiom of foundation, but this does not mean "the set of all sets" is a problematic expression in every possible system. Similarly, the problem for the set of all sets that arises from Cantor's theorem that the power set of a set X always has a greater cardinality than X can be circumvented in different ways, not all of them committed to the claim that "the set of all sets" is an empty symbol.

This is apparent from Kant's example of the expression "the age of the universe." Attributing an age to the universe is an illusion in Kant's analysis, and yet modern astrophysics deals with the universe as with any other physical object, and ascribes an age to it. Thus, an expression that has no reference in one theory has a reference in another. The problem

---

[3] And this is true even if we generally admit that we have no set theory at present that is superior to ZFC.

is not that Kant chose a bad example for demonstrating illusions, but rather that his analysis is not precise and needs to be amended.

Illusions in set theory should be dealt with similarly. Both of the approaches to explaining illusions in set theory see them as mistakes. The first sees it as a mistake we have a tendency to make, and the other that we are led to this mistake by the structure of reason. But the fact that paradoxes can be resolved in a number of ways, and that in some of them the expression at issue turns out to be meaningful while in other cases it turns out not to be, indicates that the illusion leading to the paradox is not a mistake at all, or at least it is not merely a mistake.

I wish to present a picture that is a refinement of DP. It is not the case that sentences or expressions can be divided into those that are acceptable and those that are not. In the light of what I showed in the previous chapter, it would be better to consider some linguistic expressions as "inchoate," thus dividing all the expressions into three categories. An expression A is considered "inchoate" if the question "Is there something that is A?" is an inchoate question. For example, the question "Is there a set that is the set of all sets?" or "Is the collection of all sets a set?" is an inchoate question, and therefore "The set of all sets" is an inchoate expression.

Thus, instead of drawing the conclusion that some expressions that we thought were meaningful are actually meaningless, or that some laws that we considered absolute are not valid in certain cases, we can make a more refined judgment. We do not have to say that the existence of a paradox showed us that an expression such as "the set of all sets" is actually meaningless. Rather, we can say that certain paradoxes, such as Russell's paradox, help us realize that certain expressions are inchoate.

The view that emerges here can be given the following description. A certain set theory develops the expression "set of all sets" as a referring expression by constituting it this way, while another theory shows that the promise of this expression cannot be fulfilled, and judges it as lacking reference.

As a first approximation, this situation is analogous to the case where we have an expression $h(a)$, and we manage to show that for theories S and T, we have $F(S, h(a) = X)$ but $F(T, h(a) = b)$. This view is not really formalized here, and perhaps it cannot be formalized rigorously, but it enables us to understand better what we have here.

We see that important aspects of set theory and the foundations of mathematics are dominated by non-arbitrary expansions from finite sets. But given our experience with expansions so far, there is no reason to assume that there is a single set theory that naturally arises through this process. The multiplicity of set theories is therefore not a surprising outcome.

In terms of the concept of construction introduced in chapter 6, this suggestion means that we are not mistaken about facts that exist in some Platonic world. This world is entirely constructed by our projections. Paradoxes demonstrate the failure or collapse of an attempt at constructing a particular space, not that one of our beliefs is false or that one expression is meaningless.

This last characterization allows us to amend the analogy between an expression like "the set of all sets" and the expression "the square root of -1." The first approximation that I suggested above maintained that the various sets are non-arbitrary expansions, projections from our concept of a finite set. I am thus drawing a strong analogy between the various set theories and the expansion of the power function to the zero. I am claiming that the debates between the proponents of different set theories are analogous to the debates between Bernoulli, Leibniz, and Euler that I discussed in chapter 1 above.

But even though this analogy seems correct as a first approximation, there are still some differences between set theories and other expansions. In cases where we expand a function, we know we are doing so. The question of what $\log(-1)$ is might strikes us as odd before we perform the expansion and the question of "What is 2 to the power of 0?" goes against the definition of the power function. The claim that the collection of all sets is a set, however, does not seem to be an expansion at all; it sounds like an ordinary assertion. We might, though, say that this appearance is deceiving, and that the expression "the set of all sets" really is an inchoate expression (not a meaningless one), and this indeed is my claim. From this standpoint I accept a great deal of Kant's analysis. Still, I think there is a point in answering the question of why there seems to be a difference between set theories and non-arbitrary expansions. In the case of "$\log(-1)$" that we have been discussing, the strangeness of the situation is clear, since the logarithm function was not defined for negative numbers, so that we know that expressions like "$\log(-1)$" cannot have any reference. In the case of set theory, however, we do not know this; we do not know that the expression "the set of all sets" does not actually denote a set. On the contrary, we seem to have a ready-made expansion that tells us that the sentence "the set of all sets is a set" is actually an analytic sentence. Thus, to think that "the set of all sets is a set" is true is not to make a simple mistake, but to think that either "the set of all sets is a set" is true or "the set of all sets is a set" is not true is a simple mistake – one that does not take seriously the place that expansions play in the foundations of mathematics.

Thus our correction implies that, when a paradox arises, our mistake is not in expanding laws beyond their accepted sphere. This whole book is a description of the expansion of laws beyond where they were (previously) accepted, and there is no problem with that. But as I have attempted to make clear, a formal system was constructed where a seemingly innocent expression like "the sets of all sets" appeared to have a reference, but in time contradictions were found, which destroyed this construction. Nevertheless we need not infer that this expression is meaningless, or that it lacks a reference; rather, it is just inchoate.

A paradox does not alert us to a mistake we have made, but rather to the fact that when we expand our basic laws in a non-arbitrary way we may end up with two or more natural expansions that are incompatible with one another. In the present case one non-arbitrary expansion leads to the belief that there cannot be any set that is greater than the set of all sets, yet Cantor's diagonal argument leads us to the opposite conclusion. This is not a mere psychological illusion, however – it is a rational move, to the extent that all non-arbitrary expansions are rational moves.[4]

FREGE'S DISCOMFORT

Frege was never comfortable with any of the ways that were proposed for solving Russell's paradox, even after some of the axiom systems were well developed.[5] I would like to present a reconstruction of the reasons for Frege's discomfort, which involve several of his demands on logical investigations.[6]

---

[4] The comparison with Quine is beneficial: by all traditional standards of reasoning there is nothing wrong with the derivation that leads to the contradiction "An antinomy, however, packs a surprise that can be accommodated by nothing less than a repudiation of part of our conceptual heritage" (Quine 1977, pp. 4–9). In the terminology I am using here Quine requires ad hoc contractions of extensions of concepts. I agree that paradoxes are not simple mistakes, and that the derivation of a paradox is a natural application of logical laws, but the entire space where the paradox lies is constituted by expansions. It follows that when we suggest a theory to avoid the paradox we are not suggesting an ad hoc correction, and the problem that the paradoxes reveal is therefore less acute.

[5] This idea was pointed out to me by Gilead Bar-Elli.

[6] Dummett held that Russell's paradox destroys Frege's entire philosophical project. The main point of this project was the introduction of numbers as objects by supplying the identity conditions between them, as Frege showed in his *Foundations of Arithmetic*. But this methodology was found problematic in the *Grundgesetze*: axiom V also introduces objects by presenting identity conditions, but it leads to a paradox. This shows, according to Dummett, that Frege's entire notion is problematic. The problem I see here in Frege's view is compatible with the one Dummett sees, although it is more general.

First, Frege had an idea that can be expressed as the claim that "logic is our home." A logic which is threatened by doubt or the possibility of contradiction is not worthy of its name. Logic is the basis upon which our concepts of truth and falsity are constructed. Thus, even though propositions in logic are informative, they have a special status. While we have no difficulty in maintaining a proposition in physics while thinking that it may be false, we cannot hold a logical system yet claim that we may be mistaken with regard to it.[7]

In this view any attempt to prove the consistency of a logical system is evidence that the system is not a logical one, as both the concept of proof and the concept of consistency presuppose the existence of logic. This idea seems natural, as it would obviously be absurd to try to prove the consistency of modus ponens. I shall return to this idea later in this chapter.

There are several pieces of evidence for attributing this view to Frege. One of them is the following:

This contradiction comes like a thunderbolt from a clear sky. How could we be prepared for anything like this in exact logic? Who can go surety for it that we shall not suddenly encounter a contradiction as we go on? The *possibility* [my emphasis] of such a thing points to a mistake in the original design ... This expedient [Schroeder's theory of types], as it were, belatedly gets the ship off the sandbank; but if she had been properly steered, she could have been kept off it altogether (quoted in Dummett 1973, p. 664).

This citation tells us that Frege saw his work as an attempt to eliminate the possibility that any contradictions could arise.

We should also consider the concept of possibility we are using when we deny the possibility that a contradiction may arise. If a system is consistent, then in every metaphysical sense it is impossible to discover a contradiction. In the above citation Frege says much more than merely that a logical system should have no contradictions. He also seems to be demanding that any adequate logical system must be guaranteed to be free from any contradictions. In this sense, Frege requires much more from logic than from physics.

Frege also discusses the impossibility of illusions in logic in his later writings, where he rejects the analogy between perceptual and logical

---

[7] There is an aspect of this that was developed in Wittgenstein's *Tractatus*, and which is implicit in Kant's view of logic. One attempt to explain it can be found in Putnam (1994).

illusions. There too he asserts that logic is "wholly inside us" (Frege 1979, p. 269). This assertion should not be understood as psychologism on Frege's part. Any formal system that contains doubts or the suspicion of a paradox is not a true logic. This is not only because any system that is not certain cannot be called logic, but also for a more fundamental reason. Logic assumes a notation, in which every signifier has its appropriate signified. Before we can apply the laws of logic to a particular language, we must assume that the language exists as an appropriate sign system.

This requirement of Frege's is very concrete: every expression that is supposed to denote something actually does so, while any expression that is not supposed to denote anything is outside the realm of logic. Here we again encounter what we have already seen – that proper names which do not denote objects, or predicates which are not defined everywhere, may be meaningful, but they belong to fiction rather than science. It seems to me that the ubiquity of this simple requirement should be seen as confirming the depth of Frege's thought. It is so basic that we cannot begin to formulate a logic without it. This is a problem that is uncovered by the paradoxes, which returns us to the expression, "Our language misled us." Frege puts it this way:

One feature of language that threatens to undermine the reliability of thinking is its tendency to form proper names to which no objects correspond. If this happens in fiction, this has no detrimental effect. It's different if it happens in a statement which makes the claim to be strictly scientific ... From this has arisen the paradoxes of set theory which have dealt the death blow to set theory itself ... I myself was under this illusion when in attempting to provide a logical foundation for numbers, I tried to construe numbers as sets. It is difficult to avoid an expression that has universal currency, before you learn of the mistakes it can give rise to. *It is extremely difficult, perhaps impossible* [my emphasis], to test every term offered to us by language to see whether it is logically innocuous. So a great part of the work of a philosopher consists – or at least ought to consist – in a struggle against language (Frege 1979, pp. 269–70).

I believe that what Frege is saying here is that it is impossible to do logic without the assumption that we possess a modicum of acceptable expressions. But distinguishing between acceptable and unacceptable expressions is very "difficult, perhaps impossible," and it is not certain that we have any way of doing so. Therefore logic cannot get started, and the very notion of thought becomes problematic.

For a moment, though, it seems that Frege (1979) has solved the problem. He suggests making a distinction between language and thought, and placing the onus on language:

Thus if we . . . attend instead to the true nature of thinking, we shall not be able to equate it with speaking. In that case we shall not derive thinking from speaking; thinking will then emerge as that which has priority and we shall not be able to blame thinking for the logical defects we have noted in language (ibid.).

Frege has practically no alternative. I shall try to justify this claim.

The possibility of blaming thought, claiming that it has misled us, is not open to him. Kant's analysis of the source of metaphysical illusions led him to believe that what deceives us is not our imagination but reason itself. Frege cannot accept this view, as he considers thoughts to be in the realm of the signified. We can even go further and explain that Frege's notion of a thought is directed at the world. If it has no connection with the world, it is not a thought, so the idea of a misleading thought is incoherent.

The only thing Frege can claim is that a certain linguistic expression has misled us and caused us to think that it is the object of a thought when it actually is not, because one of the components of the expression is not a signifier. In other words, it is language that deceived us. Yet Frege does seem to sense that there is a problem here. Philosophers are supposed to take care of the connection between language and thought, thus avoiding illusions. But this is not entirely obvious: "How is it possible for thinking to be engaged in a struggle with speaking? Wouldn't that be a struggle in which thinking was at war with itself? Doesn't this spell out the end to the possibility of thinking?" (ibid.). Here Frege is momentarily defending the possibility of logic, but he raises a problem which he does not see as a simple one. Where can the distinction be made between meaningful expressions that denote objects and expressions that do not denote objects? How can we explain the fact that an expression does indeed denote an object? Is the arena in which the discussion takes place inside or outside of logic? Does it occur in language or in thought? How can we know that we are not being misled here?

I think that such problems indicate that something went wrong here with Frege's basic principles – not only because Frege did not offer a way to solve these problems, but because I am not sure that these are good questions at all. It seems to me that what involved Frege in difficulties was the problem of deciding what is "within language" and what is "within thought." It is not clear how one can defend thought by putting the blame on language for all difficulties in logic. The paradoxes did indeed raise questions about Frege's paradigm for investigating thought. Another way of saying this is that Frege thought that logic must be the basis of everything, but in order for it to begin there must be some guarantee that certain conditions will be satisfied, and the natural candidate for checking these conditions is logic itself, which leads to an infinite regress. If we consider the fact that we are continually expanding and changing our concepts, then we can easily see why it is impossible to wait until all our concepts are formed before we can begin to investigate logic.

AMENDING FREGE'S POSITION

It seems at first glance that it might be possible to solve Russell's paradox by proposing a system in which this paradox does not arise, with the hope that we might find a proof of the relative consistency of this system. If we can do this for a formal system similar to Frege's, then we would seem to have solved the problem.[8]

In light of what we have just written, however, this clearly cannot be a complete solution for Frege's discomfort and pessimistic outlook. First of all, according to the view suggested here, Frege's pessimism involves not only set theory, but a much broader area. The problem of guaranteeing an object for every name goes far beyond set theory. Frege discusses at length the example of "the concept of 'horse,'" which on the one hand denotes an object (because of the definite description), yet on the other hand is a concept.

Second, it is doubtful that the way people currently respond to the paradox problem would allow us to allay Frege's discomfort. One of Frege's goals in studying logic was his aim to be free of the problems in natural language and to design a language for thought. A logical system, however, is not considered a language for thought only because it has clear construction rules and uses symbols that are not used in natural language. A system is logical in the narrow sense if it is guaranteed that every expression which is supposed to denote something actually does.

---

[8] Such an achievement can be credited to Boolos (1986). He proposed an elegant change to the system Frege had put forward in his *Grundgesetze der Arithmetik*, to create a system in which arithmetic can be formulated. More specifically, arithmetic can be developed in second-order logic from a new version of axiom V. Boolos also succeeded in proving that his new version, which avoids Russell's paradox, is consistent if second-order logic is. Boolos is well aware that this system cannot save Frege's logicism.

If this cannot be guaranteed, then, at least on my reading of Frege, we have an expansion of natural language rather than a logical system. We are in the space of speech rather than thought.

Third, the consistency of a system is not enough, at least according to Frege, to prove that expressions which seem to denote something do indeed refer to something, and that predicates which seem to denote concepts actually do so, where the concepts are defined for every object in the world. Indeed, Frege could not even understand why set theory, which is part of logic, should be defended by a consistency proof. Logic is the ground for all proofs, and to secure it by a proof is to misunderstand it. We may ask, then, whether another defense against Frege's pessimism can be found.

The phenomenon of paradoxes showed us that guaranteeing that a notation is adequate is no easy matter. However, the impossibility of providing a criterion for distinguishing between acceptable and unacceptable expressions does not imply that there is no difference between them. It may be suggested at this point that a hypothetical notion of logic could be adopted. If the expressions in the language under consideration have reference and denote thoughts, then the logic is indeed correctly applied and can be said to be true; otherwise, we merely have something that resembles logic. In the latter case the laws do not apply to anything and thus are not logical at all. The study of logic would become hypothetical, based on the assumption that its expressions actually do denote something. Frege would clearly have totally rejected such a logic, as he was extremely strict in his requirements for what logic should be. He believed that an argument is not a logical one in the full sense of the word unless the premises are true. Otherwise, he claimed, it is not a logical argument.

I suggested earlier in this chapter that the unambiguous DP is wrong. This implies that Frege's belief that it will never be possible to find a way of classifying expressions as acceptable or unacceptable (through the distinction between expressions with and without reference) is based on an invalid assumption. When we consider superstructures such as set theory, this classification is not exhaustive. We must therefore conclude that the requirement that logic can only be done after all expressions have been classified into two groups was inappropriate in the first place.

Frege wanted to force all expressions to be classified as denoting or non-denoting, and when he saw that some expressions would not obey his wish he became pessimistic about logic in general. But from the present viewpoint the very question of whether an expression such as "the set of all sets" or even "the universe" is of the same type as "Eve's oldest son" or "Adam's father" is not a good question. The difficulty in making this classification is inherent in the nature of such expressions.

To be sure, classifying expressions into three categories may be quite difficult. An expression may seem to belong to the category of those without reference, but later on it may turn out that it can be given a reference (as in the case of "the square root of −1"). Moreover, an expression may seem to have a reference, such as "the set of all sets," but later on it may turn out to be inchoate. Yet this proposal has actually improved our situation considerably, for when we tried to classify all expressions into two categories we were searching for the impossible, while now we are merely searching for something difficult to find.

This difference should lift Frege's despair. After all, Frege believed that an expression of the form "the so-and-so" is actually a proper name, in contrast to Russell, who considered such an expression incomplete. What Frege requires for logical investigation is that in order to find out if such an expression is acceptable we must check whether or not it actually has a unique reference. An investigation of this sort is, however, likely to be extremely difficult. For example, I do not know if the expression "Churchill's oldest daughter" denotes an object or not, and I can mistakenly think that such an expression denotes an object even if it actually does not. Yet it was not the difficulty of finding out whether such expressions have a reference that led Frege to despair. And if this problem did not lead Frege to be doubtful about the possibility of logic, then there is no reason for the difficulty of classifying expressions into three categories to make us pessimistic about it.

Frege did not even require that every expression of the form "the so-and-so" should be decidable as to whether it denotes a unique object or not. In fact, due to our present understanding of undecidability, we now know that in some cases we have no way of finding this out. What Frege did require was that every expression subject to deduction rules should be a denoting expression. If we are given a sentence of the form "the so-and-so is X," we must find out if the expression "the so-and-so" actually denotes an object.

There is no problem, however, in understanding how logic, with some additional assumptions, can help us find this out: after proving that there is only one object for which the predicate $P(x)$ holds, we can use the expression "the P." We thus avoid the complications discussed in the previous section, which led Frege to declare a war between logic and language.

An interesting question here is whether there is an analogy between referring expressions and what Frege would see as misleading expressions. Specifically, we are asking whether logic, in the broad sense of the word used in this book, can be used to determine whether an expression is inchoate or not, thereby avoiding the problems that plagued Frege.

Let me expand this idea. We begin our logical investigation with a tentative classification of expressions into those that obviously denote objects and those that clearly do not. The former category includes expressions such as "Churchill," while the latter includes expressions such as "Adam's father." Another category of expressions, such as "the set of all sets," "This sentence is true," and "the set of natural numbers," is controversial. Some people, relying on "the light of reason," place them in the first category, while others place them in the second. However, everyone agrees that there are expressions that clearly belong to one of the two categories and others that are problematic. This agreement can be tested empirically: we can ask people to sort such expressions as "Clinton," "Macbeth," "the center of gravity of the universe," "the cause of itself," "the last sentence Wittgenstein wrote," and "the age of the universe," and they will sort them into three categories in this way.

Along with these three categories, there is another category of evident expressions, which are generally called axioms. This category includes statements such as "Every object either belongs or does not belong to a given set," "The whole is greater than any of its parts," "The identity relation is transitive," "Every object can in principle be given a name," or "No object can be in two places at the same time." At some stage, however, there begins a sort of struggle between the problematic expressions and the axioms. The axioms carry such conviction that we are sure they must include all expressions in their sway, yet the problematic expressions have a peculiar complexity that was not noticed when the axioms were formulated. It was the paradoxes that taught us to be especially careful with expressions of this sort. Nothing seems more certain than the statement "Every sentence is either true or false," yet the expression "This sentence is false" belies this law.

This struggle between the axioms and the problematic expressions can be resolved in a variety of ways. We can give up one of the axioms and declare that we were mistaken when we thought it was always true of every object, and that actually it is valid only for a limited range of objects (for example, the finite objects in the case of the axiom "The whole is greater than any of its parts"). Or we might say that some problematic expression does not actually denote any object, so that the inapplicability of the axiom in this case is not a difficulty (as in the case of "1 divided by 0" not invalidating the laws of algebra). Sometimes we may not be able to make a final decision in the case of a specific problem. We could construct a system in which the expression would not have a reference and the axioms would be preserved, or we could construct a reference for the expression and give up some of the axioms.

This struggle between the laws and the problematic expressions is at least partly a competition between non-arbitrary expansions. The conflict between the attempt to attribute numbers to infinite sets and the claim that this must be avoided because the whole must always be greater than any of its parts was basically a debate about different expansions of the concept of number to infinite sets. This debate was resolved in the same way as most debates about forced expansions: one solution was found to be more interesting and fruitful than the other. But it is unnecessary for such debates to be resolved in a particular way, just as the question of how to expand a given concept can remain open, even though we may have a number of appropriate answers to the question.

I have said that expressions like "the universe" and "the age of the universe" are inchoate. Kant believed that the universe was not an object, supporting this claim with the argument that the concept of age cannot be expanded to include it. But this support, like the principles of Kant's critique, was insufficient to decide how such expression would be viewed. Modern astrophysics has shown us how to deal with such expressions and refute Kant's arguments by giving the expressions a meaning. Kant thought he had proven that such expressions do not refer to anything by appealing to his antinomies, but he did not realize that his view is (at best) only one among many non-arbitrary ways of speaking about the age of the universe. To use an expression defined in chapter 3 above, modern astrophysics has shown us that this particular expansion of Kant's is not strongly forced.[9]

In this reading, expressions such as "our language misled us" or "reason misled us" can be understood in a non-worrying way. At first glance

---

[9] From a logical viewpoint, the question of the age of the universe is apparently meaningless due to the special theory of relativity, which claims that questions about the age of anything cannot be given an absolute answer because they depend on the relativistic system in which they are asked. But the distribution of matter in the universe, being an empirical state, allows us to answer this question. We are asking the question from the viewpoint of systems in which the distribution of mass in the universe is more or less homogeneous, and it turns out that in all these systems there is one unique answer to the question. In some other possible worlds the question about the age of the universe might well be meaningless.

we might think that an expression such as "the set of all sets" is a totally acceptable expression denoting an object. When we are then confronted with a proof that "the set of all sets" is greater than itself, we find ourselves in a dilemma, as a result of which we say "our language misled us." But this is not a refutation of logic, because we can describe the situation differently. We can say that a forced expansion of certain laws necessitates that the expression denotes an object (the axiom of comprehension), while Cantor's expansion of the proposition that the power set of any set is greater than the set itself, so as to apply it to infinite sets, leads to a situation in which the expression "the set of all sets" is a problematic one. We can then decide to preserve Cantor's proof and claim that the collection of all sets is not a set. In doing so, we place this expression in the category of inchoate expressions rather than those that denote objects. We do not place it, however, in the category of expressions that definitely do not denote objects, because we may later decide to preserve the axiom of comprehension and reject Cantor's expansion, or something similar. Either way, the discussion can clearly be held in terms of forced expansions.

We need to use logic all the time; we cannot wait for a final, unambiguous decision about whether particular expressions denote objects or not. We have to start somewhere, so we investigate whether some given expression does or does not denote an object or is problematic, and logic plays an important role in this investigation. Similarly, we cannot wait until we have the complete set of true sentences before we start using some of them as premises in deductions. We do not need to ascertain the truth or falsity of every sentence before we can use logic; on the contrary, in many cases we must use logic in order to decide whether a sentence is true, false, or inchoate, and this is indeed one of its main uses.

The analogy that we made between discovering whether an expression is inchoate and discovering whether a definite description designates a unique object should not hide an important difference between them. In the case of definite descriptions such as "Eve's oldest son," we ask whether there is one unique object that answers this description, while in the case of inchoate expressions the question is whether it is possible to construct an object fitting a particular expression. Inchoate expressions may allow us to develop new objects, or it may turn out that no objects correspond to them, in which case we continue to call them inchoate, but in both cases we follow the same laws.

In order for the suggested emendation to be intelligible, we must assume that the speaker who was led astray by some paradox failed to distinguish between feeling certain that a particular law can be expanded to include a particular case, and knowing that the law is already true of this case. When I discussed the power function in a previous chapter, I could not decide whether the sentence "220 is greater than 219" was a forced expansion or the discovery of a truth. I only claimed that it might be the product of a forced expansion (see Epilogue). However, the phenomenon of paradoxes in set theory strongly supports the view that all talk about the structure of sets is based on non-arbitrary expansions. Indeed, this assumption explains some phenomenological features that accompany the paradoxes. This is what I deduce from the phenomenon of paradoxes, rather than the DP.

I think this view is intuitive, and some of the prime logicians of our time, like Robinson, held views very close to it. Nevertheless, it should be seen as a suggestion that must be put to the test. One of its merits is that it arises naturally from the ideas presented in this book (especially in chapters 6 and 8), and I believe it offers an improvement over the DP.

To sum up, Kant clarified the connection between antinomies and the expansion of laws beyond their legitimate range. This was the origin of the notion of the DP. My claim is that such an expansion of laws is not necessarily an improper move. On the contrary, all of modern science rests on this operation. However, the paradoxes show that sometimes a space which we considered to be a set of truths about an objective world independent of us is actually a product of construction. For such a space of expressions even the claim that some expression is meaningless is actually a type of construction.[10]

---

[10] This discussion is actually an attempt to combine two separate attempts of Frege's to deal with the paradox according to his views. Before he presented his amendment to the fifth axiom, Frege attempted to resolve the paradox through changes in syntax and ontology. He was prepared to investigate the possibility of obtaining a category of improper objects, but he rejected this idea. Later he suggested a category of sham proper names, but he rejected that as well. The former category was meant to include objects that are not exactly real, while the second was meant to include proper names that are not names (see Frege 1977a, pp. 234–44)). The idea of misleading expressions is close to both of these ideas.

How do we go on from here?

In this book I have analyzed a certain type of expansion of concepts – non-arbitrary changes of extension – and investigated some implications for the philosophy of language and of mathematics. I hope that I have managed to prove my central claim about the importance of the phenomenon of expansions to fundamental questions in mathematics and logic. But I am far from believing the interest in this phenomenon is exhausted in this book. In fact, since my interest here was to present forced expansions, and their relevance to important questions that have been discussed in philosophy since Frege, I have not exhausted the subjects discussed in the previous nine chapters. Instead of summarizing what I have presented so far, I wish to illustrate the directions in which the phenomenon of conceptual change should be researched.

I present the simplest issues first and work my way up to the more difficult ones.

A. Modern logic, founded by Frege, gives us no tools for understanding concept development, for it forces us to claim of the developed concept that either it is identical to the old one or it is completely different from it. When we get to philosophy, we feel that this sharp division is insufficient to get to the bottom of the problem, but dealing with a specific problem of this sort does not let us return to logic, or to simpler situations and to see what happens there. The first cluster of questions I propose is to take examples of expansions from mathematics and science, preferably as simple as possible, and to analyze them. Thus, removed from the heat of the philosophical debate we are discussing, we can see what is happening in a clearer way.[1]

---

[1] To see how controversial a debate that touches on expansions can be, one may recall the question of whether abortion is "really" murder, or a "mere" expansion of the concept of murder.

This mission is divided into two: one, the collection of examples of the phenomenon of expansions from science and mathematics; and two, a presentation of an analysis, categorization, and generalization of these expansions. Examples for the first part are the move from complex numbers to quaternions, the application of the notion of derivative to all spaces $\mathbb{R}^k$ with a complex Borel measure (see Rudin 1966, p. 164 for a clear definition), the different definitions of series convergence (one such definition says that, for example, $1 + 1 - 1 + 1 - 1 \ldots$ converges to $\frac{1}{2}$!), etc. It would be interesting to include here examples of expansions in science, such as the attribution of momentum and energy to a wave, etc.

Subsequently, an analysis must be suggested. Actually, a number of different analyses may be suggested, and then each should be shown with its pros and cons (see, for example, the analyses in chapter 6 about the expansion to the complex numbers). Thanks to such analyses, we will arrive at new expansion concepts, and escape the narrow dichotomy of the new concepts being identical or totally different from the old, due to Frege.

B. Other issues pertain to changes of concepts that do not involve changes of extension. The concept of a straight line has been changed from the Newtonian to the relativistic concept, but this does not necessarily involve a change in extension of the sort discussed in this book. Here we can ask questions such as: What is the relation between the Euclidean and the non-Euclidean straight line? Is their name the only thing they have in common? Is it possible to discuss these changes in the light of the analysis presented here? How can we describe the transition from the intuitive concept of a number to a Fregean concept or the concept suggested by set theory? Discussions of these questions lead to classical issues such as the nature of scientific revolutions, and what explication is.

C. Another group of questions asks to what extent we can use the structure of forced expansions to help us on specific issues in the various sciences. I do not mean using this structure to describe the methodology or logic of science, but rather as a tool or part of the language of particular sciences. For example, can we use the structure of expansions to describe language acquisition? Or to describe the phenomenon of filling in blind spots in vision? Can we provide a set theory that is based not on the predicate calculus but on the logic of expansions?

Some other questions involve logical discussions that may not be as basic as those just mentioned but are still very important. For example, to what extent could moral dilemmas be analysed in terms of forced expansions? Is a dilemma a situation in which we have forced expansions of different ethical principles which turn out to be incompatible with one another? Is this enough to refute the arguments sometimes offered in discussions of dilemmas, which claim that dilemmas are logically impossible because any true dilemma must involve an act which is both right and wrong at one and the same time? Can the discussion of the expansions of concepts contribute to our understanding of such topics as analogies, metaphors, or vagueness? These and similar questions deserve careful investigation. I have given examples of such possible applications throughout this book, as in my discussion of Goedel's arguments, the phenomenon of paradoxes, and the debate between Frege and the formalists.

D. Questions of the type just mentioned seem likely to lead to fruitful research. One interesting question is what happens when we try the "*forcification*" of a field of study, i.e., to see it as constituted out of non-arbitrary expansions of certain types. The basic question underlying all of them is which areas of inquiry can be seen as constituted by non-arbitrary expansions. This question is dependent on another basic question: which type of justification is likely to lead to such a conclusion?

Sometimes we can show formally that a particular area can be seen as having been obtained by means of expansions, but this is not enough to show that this space was actually constituted this way. We might be able to obtain the even numbers by an expansion of the odd numbers, but that does not mean that we have to see the natural numbers as having been obtained by expansion from the odd numbers. True, when we have a feeling that a certain structure is based on another one, and we can demonstrate this formally – as in the case of the negative numbers or the complex numbers – then this move is not only reasonable but also has a certain epistemic advantage. Nevertheless, the question of whether one area is obtained from another by expansion is rarely easy to answer.

Consider, for example, Wittgenstein's question, which I discussed in chapter 1, of whether the relation between the addition of large numbers and that of small numbers is the same as the relation between the complex numbers and the real numbers. Do we understand it better now? Are we closer to finding a satisfactory answer to it? We can see now that it is possible to see these relations according to Wittgenstein's suggestion, and it may even be possible to see every new calculation as an expansion, but what advantage do we gain by looking at the situation this way? It is not enough to use our intuition; we must bring support for assertions of this sort.

If we have a theory that explains our grasp of small numbers, then the mechanism of expansion allows us to explain the entire class of natural numbers as an expansion of the primary space we started with. Nevertheless, this is not always true. Imagine, for example, some creature who knows how to calculate the factorial function for real numbers. For such a creature this function is a primitive one. Now we can assume that even for this creature the factorial function for the natural numbers is more accessible, since there is a simple algorithm that decides every value. Can we see such a creature as one who is actually expanding this function all the time? I believe not, as this would imply that the expansion is forced by the constraints that determine the gamma function, but the creature may be unaware of this fact.

Arguments of this sort are also problematic when the operation is so elementary that seeing it as being obtained from a non-arbitrary expansion does not help us in any way. This is the case with the suggestion that every new calculation is an expansion. It is hard to believe that this could explain anything, since performing an expansion requires abilities that are unlikely to be simpler than the elementary calculations under consideration.

When we succeed in showing that our approach can also solve riddles associated with this area, we have indirect support for our claim that expansions are involved here. We make an attempt to impose the logical structure of expansions, the possibility of forced expansions that are not strongly forced within the area under discussion, and we see if the imposition is successful. If it is, and if it also solves some riddles, then we have a good basis for arguing that there is an expansion of concepts here.[2] The area of ethical dilemmas that I mentioned above is one such area. Kant's argument in *Critique of Pure Reason* based on the antinomies and the discussion of paradoxes in the previous chapter have a similar form.

In order to argue that every new calculation is a non-arbitrary expansion, it would therefore be advisable to provide riddles that could be explained by this conjecture but not by others. In the case of calculations with large numbers we can answer the question of how they are accessible, but it may be possible to answer this question in other ways as well. We might, for example, see this accessibility as an elementary logical

---

[2] It does not matter here if the area already exists independently of the forced expansion. We see the sentence "$(-3) \times (-3) = 9$" as constituted by an expansion even if there is a "-3" in some Platonic world. This is similar to the question that might be asked about what we would say about Kant's theory if we could take off our "space-time glasses" and discover that the world of things-in-themselves is exactly the same as the world of phenomena.

derivation from the definition, without the need to use the mechanism of expansion. Moreover, we would also have to check whether there are any arguments that support a reverse conclusion. For now we must leave Wittgenstein's suggestion as an open question.

E. A question that arose in this book was in what sense proofs can be seen as expansions. The question is not whether all proofs are expansions or not, but whether there are areas where the logic that is used is an expansion. When constituting a new type of mathematical space, are logical laws a projection onto that new space, akin to the projection of the commutative law in the expansion from real to complex numbers? It is noteworthy that inside a formal system proofs may be identified with calculation, and to the extent that calculations are not expansions there is no expansion here. The point I wish to raise here pertains to the constitution of a new field of study, whether the laws of logic are stretched or not.

This is not a new question, and we should note it has some different variations. According to Brouwer, classical logic is a careless expansion of logic that is basically valid for finite spaces. Hilbert thought that the validity of the law of excluded middle is due to an expansion from finite mathematics. Van Frassen also maintained that the law of excluded middle is postulated because of considerations of supervaluation. However, that entire discussion was not made in light of the phenomenon of expansions, its range and its meaning. I believe that discussing this question, like others presented in this concluding chapter, in light of the analysis presented in this book will bring about new insights. For example, if the a priori nature of logic and the existence of what Susan Haack called deviant logic can be explained from this assumption, we will have support for this thesis.

F. Another issue that should be examined is how much the idea of an inchoate thought is relative, and what it depends on. It may be possible that the question of whether a certain thought is inchoate or not depends on the theory held, or perhaps it is culture-dependent. This question ranges beyond whether the concept of inchoate thought is fuzzy or not. Let us examine a prescientific view of the creation of the universe. In this view, the proposition "the world is exactly 5,000 years old" may be grasped as a proposition that cannot be decided by any expansion. The speaker here may see age as a concept that a priori applies to himself and the universe in the same sense, i.e., that it is decided by asking older people, and not by proposing cosmological models that are an expansion of the physical behavior of everyday objects.

This question can be continued beyond prescientific positions. Assume the different methods of determining the age of the universe stabilize and converge. Does a child growing in a society where this has happened see the expression "age of the universe" as something that is in no way different from "my age"? This can have an analogy to mathematical functions: the power function can be taught as a function that is a priori defined for any complex number. In that case, there would be no expansion of the power function (at least for numbers).

This question should not be answered by showing ambiguity, i.e., just because in one society the concept of the age of the universe can be readily determined, and in another society it is arrived at through expansions, we can conclude that the proposition "the age of the universe is 5,000 years" is ambiguous. This approach might preserve the coherence of the category of inchoate thoughts, and its independence from theory and culture. But in rejecting the reference to ambiguity, I am not saying that the expression "the age of the universe" has the same meaning in both cultures. Although I do not hold a definition for meaning, I do feel that this expression has a different meaning in different cultures; but this does not say enough: one of the consequences of this book is that describing things as having "same/different meanings," or "indicating another concept," is not saying much: we want to know what kind of difference.

References

Ahlfors, L. V. (1979), *Complex Analysis*. McGraw-Hill, Singapore.

Benacerraf, P. (1983), "What Numbers Could Not Be." In *Philosophy of Mathematics*, ed. P. Benacerraf and H. Putnam. Cambridge University Press, Cambridge.

(1996), "What Mathematical Truth Could Not Be – I." In *The Philosophy of Mathematics Today*, ed. M. Schirn. Clarendon Press, Oxford.

Boolos, G. (1986), "Saving Frege from Contradiction." *Proceedings of the Aristotelian Society*, 87, pp. 137–51.

Buzaglo, M. (forthcoming), *Solomon Maimon's Metaphysics: A Reconstruction*. Pittsburgh University Press, Pittsburgh.

Crowe, M. (1992), "Ten 'Laws' Concerning Patterns of Change in the History of Mathematics." Reprinted in *Revolutions in Mathematics*, ed. Donald Gillies. Clarendon Press, Oxford.

Diamond, C. (1995), *The Realistic Spirit*. MIT Press, Cambridge MA.

Dummett, M. (1973), *Frege: Philosophy of Language*. Duckworth, London.

(1978), "The Justification of Deduction." Reprinted in *Truth and Other Enigmas*. Duckworth, London, pp. 290–318.

Fine, K. (1985), *Reasoning with Arbitrary Objects*. Basil Blackwell, Oxford.

van Frassen, B. C. (1966), "Singular Terms, Truth-Value Gaps, and Free Logic." *Journal of Philosophy*, 63.

(1978), "Rejoinder: On a Kantian Conception of Language." In *Paradox of the Liar*, ed. R. L. Martin. Ridgeview Publishing Company, California, pp. 59–66.

Frege, G. (1977a), *Grundgesetze der Arithmetik*, trans. P. E. B. Jourdain and J. Stachelroth. In *Translations from the Philosophical Writings of G. Frege*, ed. P. Geach and M. Black, Basil Blackwell, Oxford.

(1977b), "Negation." In *Translations from the Philosophical Writings of G. Frege*, ed. P. Geach and M. Black. Basil Blackwell, Oxford.

(1979), *Posthumous Writings*, ed. H. Hermes, F. Kambartel, and F. Kaulbach. University of Chicago Press, Chicago.

(1980), *Foundations of Arithmetic*. Northwestern University Press, Chicago.

(1984), *Collected Papers on Mathematics, Logic and Philosophy*, ed. B. McGuinness. Basil Blackwell, Oxford.

Gibson, J. J. (1950), *The Perception of the Visual World*. Houghton Mifflin, Boston.

Gödel, K. (1983a), "What is Cantor's Continuum Problem?" In *Philosophy of Mathematics*, ed. P. Benacerraf and H. Putnam. Cambridge University Press, Cambridge, pp. 447–69.

(1983b), "Russell's Mathematical Logic." In *Philosophy of Mathematics*, ed. P. Benacerraf and H. Putnam. Cambridge University Press, Cambridge, pp. 470–86.

Gupta, H. (1968), "On the Rule of Existential Specification in Systems of Natural Deduction." *Mind*, 77, pp. 96–103.

Hankel, H. (1867), *Theorie der complexen Zahlen Systeme*. Klein.

Hilbert, D. (1983), "On the Infinite." In *Philosophy of Mathematics*, ed. P. Benacerraf and H. Putnam. Cambridge University Press, Cambridge, pp. 183–206.

Hintikka, J. (1965), "Are Logical Truths Analytic?" *Philosophical Review*, 74, pp. 178–203.

(1967), "Kant on the Mathematical Method." *The Monist*, 51, pp. 352–75.

(1969), "On Kant's Notion of Intuition (*Anschauung*)." In *The First Critique*, ed. Terence Penelhum and J. J. MacIntosh. Wadsworth, Belmont.

(1972), "Kantian Intuitions." *Inquiry*, 15, pp. 341–5.

Hofstadter, D. (1995), *Fluid Concepts and Creative Analogies*. Basic Books, Harper Collins, New York.

Kant, I. (1933), *Critique of Pure Reason*, trans. N. Kemp Smith. London.

Kitcher, P. (1989) "Innovation and Understanding in Mathematics." *Journal of Philosophy*, October, pp. 563–4.

Klein, F. (1939), *Elementary Mathematics from an Advanced Standpoint: Arithmetic, Algebra, Analysis*. Dover, New York.

Kline, M. (1972), *Mathematical Thought from Ancient to Modern Times*, 3 vols. Oxford University Press, Oxford.

Kripke, S. (1975), "Outline to a Theory of Truth." *Journal of Philosophy*, 72, pp. 690–716.

(1982), *Wittgenstein on Rules and Private Language*. Basil Blackwell, Oxford.

Lakatos, I. (1976), *Proofs and Refutations*. Cambridge University Press, Cambridge.

(1978), *Philosophical Papers*, ed. J. Worrall and G. Currie, 2 vols. Cambridge University Press, Cambridge.

Lemmon, E. J. (1961), "Quantifier Rules and Natural Deduction." *Mind*, 70, pp. 235–8.

Maimon, S. (1965), *Gesammelte Werke*, vols. I–VII. Georg Olms Verlagsbuchhandlung, Hildesheim.

Maddy, P. (1990), *Realism in Mathematics*. Oxford University Press, Oxford.

Manders, K. (1989), "Domain Extension and the Philosophy of Mathamatics." *Journal of Philosophy*, pp. 553–62.

Mikenberg, I. (1977), "From Total to Partial Algebras." In *Mathematical Logic, Proceedings of the First Brazilian Conference*, ed. A. Arruda, N. C. A. de Costa, and R. Chuaqui, Dekker, pp. 203–23.

Parsons, C. (1979–80), "Mathematical Intuition." *Proceedings of the Aristotelian Society*, 80, pp. 145–68.

(1995), "Platonism and Mathematical Intuition in Kurt Gödel's Thought." *Bulletin of Symbolic Logic*, 1(1), pp. 44–75.

(1998), "Reason and Intuition." *Synthese*, 125(3), pp. 239–315.

Peacock, G. (1834), "Report on the Recent Progress and Present State of Certain Branches of Analysis." In *Report on the Third Meeting of the British Association for the Advancement of Science, 1833*. London, pp. 185–352.

Putnam, H. (1975a), "It Ain't Necessarily So." Reprinted in *Philosophical Papers*, vol. I, Cambridge University Press, Cambridge, pp. 237–50.

(1975b), "The Logic of Quantum Mechanics." In *Philosophical Papers*, vol. I, Cambridge University Press, Cambridge, pp. 174–97.

(1994), "Rethinking Mathematical Necessity." In *Words and Life*, Harvard University Press, Cambridge MA, pp. 245–63.

Quine, W. V. (1977), *The Ways of Paradox and Other Essays*. Harvard University Press, Cambridge MA.

Robinson, A. (1955), *Complete Theories*. North-Holland, Amsterdam.

Rudin, W. (1966), *Real and Complex Analysis*. Tata McGraw-Hill, New Delhi.

Russell, B. (1919), *Introduction to Mathematical Philosophy*, George Allen and Unwin, London.

(1956), "On Denoting." In *Logic and Knowledge*, ed. R. C. Marsh. George Allen and Unwin, London.

Steiner, M. (1998), *The Applicability of Mathematics as a Philosophical Problem*. Harvard University Press, Cambridge MA.

Wang, H. (1996), *A Logical Journey: From Gödel to Philosophy*, MIT Press, Cambridge MA.

Wilson, M. (1995), "Frege: The Royal Road from Geometry." *Nous*, 26, 1992, pp. 149–80. Reprinted in *Frege's Philosophy of Mathematics*, ed. W. Demopoulos. Harvard University Press, Cambridge MA, pp. 108–49.

Wittgenstein, L. (1953), *Philosophical Investigations*. Basil Blackwell, Oxford.

(1967), *Remarks on the Foundation of Mathematics*, trans. G. E. M. Anscombe. Basil Blackwell, Oxford.

(1974), *Philosophical Grammar*, trans. A. Kenny. Basil Blackwell, Oxford.

(1988), *Tractatus Logico-Philosophicus*, trans. C. K. Ogden. Routledge and Kegan Paul, London.

Index